About My Father's Business

The Life of Elder Michaux

LILLIAN ASHCRAFT WEBB

FOREWORD BY HENRY H. MITCHELL

CONTRIBUTIONS IN AFRO-AMERICAN AND AFRICAN STUDIES, NUMBER 61

GREENWOOD PRESS
Westport, Connecticut • London, England

Library of Congress Cataloging in Publication Data

Webb, Lillian Ashcraft.
    About my father's business.

    (Contributions in Afro-American and African Studies ;
no. 61 ISSN 0069-9624)
    Bibliography: p.
    Includes index.
    1. Michaux, Lightfoot. 2. Clergy--Washing-
ton, D. C.--Biography. 3. Washington, D. C. Church of
God (Gospel Spreading)--Biography. 4. Washington, D. C.
--Biography. I. Title. II. Series.
BX7020.Z8M528   289.9 [B]   80-24595
ISBN 0-313-22261-4 (lib. bdg.)

Library of Congress Catalog Card Number: 80-24595
ISBN: 0-313-22261-4
ISSN: 0069-9624

First published in 1981

Greenwood Press
A division of Congressional Information Service, Inc.
88 Post Road West, Westport, Connecticut 06881

Printed in the United States of America

10 9 8 7 6 5 4 3 2 1

Acknowledgment

The author and publisher are grateful for permission to quote from materials and
reprint photographs belonging to the Church of God. Used by permission of the
officers of the board of directors of the Church of God.

For
my Grandparents
and
my Parents

Contents

Illustrations

Foreword

Lillian Ashcraft Webb has added one more entry in the series of needed corrections to the image of strong black leaders in America's past. Such corrections are needed because it is still hard for the majority who manipulate America's mass media to treat with adequate accuracy and empathy any black and important figure who departs from their world. Yet if such a person is to be strong among her/his people, it will surely be necessary to be and work counter to white cultural expectations and role models. As bad as this is now, it was far worse in the days of Elder Lightfoot Solomon Michaux. Even though he had his own national radio broadcast, his image was tarnished at every turn, both by innuendo and by the selective coverage of only his most unusual activities. Dr. Webb has rendered an important service to black church history and to the history of all America.

Lillian Ashcraft Webb's credentials, academically speaking, are impressive, but one senses in addition that this work was somehow destined. She spent a part of her youth in Elder Michaux's church, and so has that crucial accuracy of an inside angle of vision. Yet

she has gone on to deal with the weightier matters of objective
research with success. One reads, thus, the work of a person with a
Ph.D. who has taught in great universities literally from coast to
coast. Configurations so felicitous are indeed infrequent.

As one who listened often to Elder Michaux nearly fifty years
ago, I have enjoyed and profited from this reading. I heartily rec-
ommend it to all serious students of Americana, especially the
black part.

Henry H. Mitchell

Acknowledgments

I express appreciation to:

Richard B. Sherman and Edward R. Crapol, both at The College of William and Mary, for direction during initial stages of this study.

Deacons Rudolph Jones and F. D. Rainey, other members and friends of the Church of God for opening doors to oral and written resources on Michaux and the church.

James H. Cone (Union Theological Seminary in New York) and my former colleagues at the University of California, Santa Barbara, for early recognition of the significance of this study and for encouraging me to complete it for publication.

Henry H. Mitchell (Director, Ecumenical Center for Black Church Studies, Los Angeles) for reading the manuscript and making valuable editorial suggestions.

My husband (James W. Webb II, founding pastor, Howard E. Thurman Institutional Church, Kansas City) who lent me a helping hand as I struggled to clarify analysis and to articulate ideas herein, and especially for his continuous understanding and patience throughout the long months of my preoccupation with this project.

Introduction

During a recent CBS "Sixty Minutes" program Mike Wallace asserted that until recently no religious groups had realized the potential use of the media for world-wide evangelism. He documented that statement with information on two groups which currently do make such use of the media. Wallace appropriately highlighted their leaders—Pat Robertson (700 Club, Virginia Beach) and Jerry Falwell (Thomas Road Baptist Church, Lynchburg, Virginia).[1]

I observed that particular program with studied interest primarily because this work on the late Elder Michaux, founder of the Church of God, Washington, D.C., was nearing completion. Similarities between Robertson, Falwell, and Michaux were striking. All three were native Virginians and each had, at different times and in different places, envisioned that the world could be evangelized via the media. The glaring dissimilarity was that Michaux, who died in 1968, had this vision in the early 1930s, almost a half century before Robertson and Falwell emerged as prominent media evangelists. Yet, Michaux's pioneering contribution toward a world-wide, media-supported evangelism remains unrecognized by students of church history as well as by the general public. My own interest in Michaux is long standing inasmuch as my youth was spent in the Church of God. Later, having matured and acquired insights suggestive of Michaux as cultist leader of a religious folk movement, I resolved to probe for a deeper intellectual understanding of this man and his church.

Although numerous articles on Michaux were available to me, their authors really had not adequately studied him. Most focused only on the most sensational aspects, such as the pageantry of his Mass Annual Baptizings, his "War on the Devil" over the radio and under big tents, his occasional prophecies and legal entanglements and his wealth and tax problems. Journalists showered the public with assorted labels that cast a negative image of Michaux as cultist, curious prophet, faith healer, millionaire, showman, object of derision, and racial conservative. This media image widely influenced opinions of the masses and to a great extent shaped scholars' interpretations of the Elder. This point is easily verified.

In 1950 a major journalist, Frank Rasky, matter-of-factly referred to Michaux as a Harlem zealot who vied with fellow cultist Mother Rosa Horne for Father Divine's abandoned territory in New York City. That article, laden with negative suggestions about Michaux and Horne, appeared in the popular *Negro Digest*.[2]

Following Rasky's lead, E. Franklin Frazier concurred in his much publicized book, *The Negro Church in America*, that the "adroit showman" indeed had struggled for "spiritual control of masses in Harlem." This millionaire, holiness preacher, with a retinue of servants and chauffeurs, had widespread popular appeal, Frazier noted. Furthermore, he "has been able to enhance his prestige by association with important public leaders some of whom . . . regard him as a spokesman for many Negro Church people." Frazier's sole documentation was the Rasky article.[3] Nevertheless, as a noted sociologist and onetime president of the prestigious American Sociological Society, his unflattering implications, based largely on popular journalism, had potential for far-reaching influence among other scholars.

The most recent treatment of Michaux adheres to the same pattern. Although Marcus Boulware's book is entitled *The Oratory of Negro Leaders: 1900-1968*, it informs us minimally about the Elder as orator. Supporting that section with a single article from the mass-oriented *Time Magazine*, Boulware arrived at a negative conclusion about

Michaux by quoting undocumented statements. "Critics of Elder Michaux," he wrote, "especially the intelligentsia admit that he was a good showman. They object, however, to his using the pulpit rather than the stage to give his show. And, most of all they scorn his injection of a 'jive' atmosphere into the Church of God."[4]

These commentaries are disconcerting both because they perpetuate a negative image of Michaux and, more importantly, because prominent "scholars" were so influenced by the media that they did not see fit to do further independent research. Fortunately, some contemporary commentators have probed deeper for details on the Elder.

Roscoe Lewis, a sociologist at Hampton Institute and editor of the Virginia Writer's Project, interviewed Michaux, his church members, business associates and other acquaintances to gather information for a short section in the book on Virginia Negroes. He also attended church and tent meetings and accompanied Michaux on rounds observing him and reactions to him. As a result, Lewis gathered valuable and little-known details that could whet appetites of curious scholars and other interested readers. He learned of Michaux's attacks on racial segregation during his early ministry, for instance, and uncovered a bit of information about his pre-Washington financial dealings. Lewis merely reported his findings without any questioning or analysis that would give credence to or rebut popular opinion.[5]

While writing his doctoral dissertation, Chancellor Williams also employed techniques of interview and observation to investigate Michaux and other leaders of religious assemblies that had emerged onto the national scene. Williams called these assemblages "storefront" churches. At this time Michaux showed him correspondence and other materials, which are no longer available, that contained potential insights into the preacher's business manuevers, his ideas concerning the relationship between church and state, and his feisty high-handedness toward entertainment "moguls" such as producers of film and theater. This resourceful manuscript is marred, however, by Williams' uncritical use of materials and interviews with Michaux and other church members. This caused him to present details without questioning them against the background of popularly held notions of the Elder.[6]

Useful leads uncovered by Lewis and Williams were available, prior to 1950, to those who would lend scholarly investigation to

their considerations of Michaux. All of these treatments, the opinion-
ated and the more scholarly and documented, contributed to this
author's better understanding of the Elder, for they were written
during Michaux's lifetime and represent the perspectives of his contemporaries. The task of those commenting on the Elder at that
time were made difficult because of the fluid state of the subject,
Michaux, whom they tried to evaluate within the context of the
1930s, 1940s, and 1950s, and because of the prevailing social thought
during those decades. Since Michaux died in 1968, he can now be
studied under more controlled conditions and with advantages of
hindsight and additional materials. Consequently, this first major
study of the Elder and his church must be more than a rejoinder to
previous writings on this subject. I am obligated to state my position
without equivocation: The conservative Michaux was so complex
in his unorthodoxy as to defy comfortable labeling and categorizing.
This removes treatment of the Elder from the level of traditionally
unquestioned popular conception to a more arguable base, especially
where discussion of him as a cultist is concerned.

My position is derived from utilizing historical methods of re-
searching to gather materials for critical evaluation. Written sources,
which historians refer to as traditional, on Michaux are scattered
from Washington to California and from the United States to England
and Haiti. Because previous accounts were so scantily documented,
they rarely were helpful guides to locating resources. There were
several useful approaches, however. The first was to become knowl-
edgeable of existing lore about the Elder. Techniques of interviewing
and engaging in informal discussions with Michaux's church members,
relatives, and associates were usually revealing mainly because
I was no stranger to them. The second step was to employ these
leads to systematically track down written sources in the National
Archives, presidential libraries, other public libraries, newspapers,
and magazines. Those sources that were in members' possession,
such as scrapbooks, photographs, newsclippings, and various me-
mentos, were placed at my disposal by authority of church officials.
Unfortunately, even materials owned by the church are scattered.

As patterns surfaced from the data, it was clear to me that an
understanding of Michaux must emerge from probing into his life,
both before and after he went to Washington. Only then could clues
to his character, experiences, theology and relationship to the tra-

ditional black church, religious folk movements, and to present-day religious corporations be made meaningful. Only then could his economic, political, and social goals, successes, and failures be assessed properly. This range of topics will be covered, for the first time, in this manuscript. As a result, Michaux's role in America's church history will unfold. Moreover, we shall be better informed of the black church in its creative variety of personalities, leadership, programs, and objectives as well as in its community of aim and expression.

I have taken these liberties in preparing this manuscript. For the sake of variety, Lightfoot, Elder Michaux, Michaux, and the Elder are used interchangeably. The Church of God still is a viable religious body, but because my interest primarily begins and ends with Michaux, today's church will be discussed only to help evaluate Michaux's success as founder and pastor. Owing to the biographical nature of this study, I thought it more logical that detailed analysis be placed in a final chapter rather than scattered at length throughout the narrative, interrupting its flow.

This study is not definitive. I have left, for example, the vast collection of Michaux's sermons, mainly tape-recorded, and economic details of his administration for others to probe and analyze. I am of the opinion, however, that any new discoveries will not basically alter my conclusions.

Finally, realizing that no one can capture verbatim nor even appreciate fully the experiences, desires, and intentions of another, I have tried to present Michaux fairly and in my interpretation to make of him neither saint nor sinner. The image presented is that of a black preacher who was complex in his unorthodoxy and conservatism. If scholars challenge my interpretation, and in so doing, increase our understanding of Michaux and his role in American church history, I shall be grateful.

About My Father's Business

1

A Special Child

You may think it unimaginative that this story actually opens with Michaux's birth. Be assured that there is no more appropriate beginning. No one else writing about Michaux has understood the significance of his birth day in relationship to his future development. The key to its significance lies in the fact that he was born with a veil covering his face. An old woman who assisted in his delivery excitedly reminded the young mother of an old wives' tale which augured that infants born with a caul, a sloughable facial covering, would have an exceptional life. That folk belief was an old one. It came from an African tradition and was identified with conjuring. During slavery it was said that only blacks born with a caul had the secret to conjuring powers.[1] Throughout his youth, Michaux's mother reminisced about how she lay and watched in awe as the midwife peeled the veil from his infant face on that Friday, November 7, 1884.[2] Hearing and retelling that incident became a family tradition. No one knew if it had occurred previously in their lineage because details pertaining to their ancestry were obscure.

The Michauxs rarely discussed ancestors on either side, so only those who remembered the forebears were privy to even the most general information. Except for a hint of ethnic lineage, the family's recordable story began with the generation that moved to Newport News, Virginia. John, Lightfoot's father, was racially mixed with French, Indian, and Negro bloodlines. John's father was a Jewish Frenchman who had immigrated to the United States and settled in the area of Richmond prior to the Civil War. There he met a woman of Negroid and Indian ancestry by whom he sired this son and at least two other children. They grew up near Richmond. When John and Henry, his younger brother, were old enough, they became merchant seamen. Many proud, young black men historically were attracted to that occupation because it was adventuresome and carried an easy interracial camaraderie and social acceptability. John and Henry cooked on a ship which sailed out of Richmond to New Orleans and New York. On its way from New Orleans it sailed into the Newport News harbor. The Michaux brothers liked what they found in that Chesapeake Bay port town. John, who already was married and had an infant son, suggested that they settle there.

When they arrived in 1883, the young husband and father found a place for his small family to live on Warwick Avenue. Their simple, poorly constructed, unpainted cottage was across from the Acre (a huge vacant field) at the edge of the Chesapeake and Ohio railroad tracks. Lightfoot was the couple's first child born on that spot. It was the best provision John could make at the time, for he had given up his job as merchant seaman and had become a struggling fish peddler in order to stay close to his family. The family grew, and John, ever ambitious and thrifty, worked long, hard hours to save money, increase customers, and expand business. Eventually, he added produce to the assortment of fish and opened a store on the main commercial street, Jefferson Avenue, amid Jewish and white gentile competitors. When Lightfoot was a young boy, the family moved into quarters above the store. The children played and worked in that commercial environment and the effect was immensely discernible in Lightfoot's life. Through a child's eye, Lightfoot saw that his father was a self-employed store-owner, presumably subservient to no one and without a "boss" or other supervisor to whom he answered. While to his doting child, John appeared to be an equal among his fellow shopkeepers within a "desegregated" islet, he could not escape the effects of racism that blanketed turn-of-the-century life. Nuances of racism limited camaraderie between blacks and whites in the commercial zone as well as accumulation of excess profit and business expansion among blacks in the area.

The children delighted in their father who, despite his busyness, was dominant in the home; they affectionately called him "Poppa."[3] John also was prominent in the black community, for he was an ambitious businessman with light skin and straight hair. Both physical characteristics then were marks of distinction, recognized and patronized by black and some white Americans until recently. This turn-of-the-century family, which carried the father's status, mingled with the "better class" of Negroes and worshipped with them at the First Baptist Church, also on Jefferson Avenue. John Michaux was well-spoken of by such prominent black folk in the area as the Fields and the Bassetts, who were influential politicians and educators in the neighboring town of Hampton.[4] The social significance of a light-skinned businessman's rather superior posture, especially in the Negro community, made a lasting imprint on young Lightfoot. He spent the rest of his life trying to ignore the crippling realities of being treated as a Negro in a white Anglo-Saxon capitalistic society despite skin color. He pursued the exclusiveness of treatment that Negroes who could "pass" frequently were accused of expecting from both white and black folk.

On the other hand, Lightfoot saw that his mother, May Blanche, a woman of dark hue and more Negroid features, was virtually unknown in the community. She concentrated on the household and on day-to-day maintenance of the ten of her fifteen children who survived infancy. Not only was she burdened with household chores and frequent pregnancies but May Blanche also was plagued by a nervous condition. In the year that Lightfoot turned twenty-one her illness worsened, and she lapsed into a nervous breakdown.[5] John sent her off to Virginia's black mental institution in Petersburg. When she recovered sufficiently to return home, marital problems either developed or intensified. It took little imagination for their children to realize that the marriage was far from ideal as tempers often flared and display of affection obviously was lack-

ing. One result of this friction was that May Blanche and John occupied separate apartments in the same building. She never recovered fully from the mental illness, and John, who had little patience, grew increasingly hostile toward her despite constant chid-
ings from Lightfoot that he should "behave" better.[6]

In spite of her weaknesses and limitations, Lightfoot's mother influenced his life significantly. She reminded him continuously that
he was her "different child," born to a special mission. Even his
name made him feel special. Lightfoot Solomon. Lightfoot—in
honor of his mother's Indian ancestry. Solomon—out of his pater-
nal grandfather's Jewish heritage, after the wise and wealthy Old
Testament King Solomon. The heightened ego matched Lightfoot's
identification with his father, whose stock the boy thought was
superior. The boy came to believe that much was expected of him,
and he acted like he was special. He had considerable moral and
religious devoutness. Unlike his brothers, he neither smoked nor
drank. He attended church regularly—on Sunday mornings to study
in the Baptist Sunday School and on Sunday nights to be a commu-
nicant in Presbyterian services. He was good natured but a loner
who kept to himself and formed no lasting friendships. He liked
girls in his classes at the black Twenty-second Street School and
sometimes he took them fruit to get their attention, hoping to capture their affection.

All too soon he cast aside the carefree days and fantasies of a
schoolboy. A compulsive personality took the ascendancy, and
Lightfoot was the child-adult constantly driven by ambition to excel.
Unfortunately, he quit school before learning to read well enough
to be comfortable in the lifestyle that he later would assume. He
went to work fulltime with his father. Each weekday Lightfoot
loaded a cart with oysters, clams, crabs, and assorted fish. He packed
them carefully in ice and pushed the cart several miles across Newport News to sell to "well-to-do white people in the north end."[7] At
that time he was about eleven.

Newport News was still largely undeveloped. There were few
paved avenues, streets, or sidewalks, and only occasional brick and
wooden walkways. It was not uncommon to see horses, goats, and
hogs trotting alongside pathways. Collis P. Huntington, idol of the
ambitious, had located the shipyard and Chesapeake and Ohio
Railroad in that city. While these industries provided many men

with jobs, they were still in the developing stage. The commercial atmosphere was laissez-faire, openly competitive, and many young men believed they could work hard, save their money, and become rich like Huntington.[8] Lightfoot was one of these ambitious youngsters. Within his mind lodged the prevailing social idea that he could attain whatever heights he desired and even overcome limitations assigned his race. He worked hard, long hours each day, and saved at the local black-operated Sons and Daughters of Peace Penny, Nickel and Dime Savings Bank, planning one day to open his own seafood and poultry store. This dream came true around 1904 when he not only hung the sign for his store, but also opened, as a sideline, a dancing school. Here he taught the Schottische and other popular dances in that period. He discovered that being enterprising paid off in more ways than money, for at the dancing school, he taught his future wife, Mary Eliza Pauline. Lightfoot thought she was beautiful with her light skin, fine features, and slightly wavy long hair. During a dance with him, she flirtingly remarked that he would make her a good husband. Theirs was not a story of love at first sight, although Lightfoot later took advantage of a "discreet" opportunity to woo her. This came one night when he saw her sobbing, sitting on the doorsteps to the rooming house where she stayed. He stopped and asked her what was wrong. Between sobs she explained that her "husband" had put her out and she had no money and no place to go. Gently he said, "If you promise to be my girl only, I'll get you a place to stay." She promised. A courtship followed, and they married around 1906.

Mary Michaux was an attractive, volatile, illiterate woman of undetermined family origins. She was orphaned at an early age, without any known relatives, and reared by a foster mother on Virginia's eastern shore. She made two boastful claims about her personal past: That her father was a white man and that she had given birth to a baby in a previous marriage. She bragged about her white father and wistfully spoke about her baby who died in infancy. About the baby she would say, "Its feet looked just like its daddy's." Separation from the baby's father, whether her husband or not, had been painful, and immediately following it Mary lived aimlessly, wantonly, and sometimes homelessly and hungry, rooming in such hovels as the one above Gresham's Bar which was in Jefferson Avenue's "redlight" district. After marrying Lightfoot, she became a fanatical convert to holiness, and the couple began attending Saint Timothy Church of Christ (Holiness), where he was selected secretary-treasurer.[9]

Mary was ambitious and complemented her husband well in financial matters with her qualities of diligence and thrift. Sometimes she was comical in her frugality, especially to the young woman secretary-clerk who worked in the store and observed that Mary collected tissue from crates of citrus fruits and she neatly stashed these away for use at home as toilet paper. Working together, she and her husband accumulated enough savings by 1911 to build a large three-story house on Ivy Avenue at Pinkey's Beach, overlooking the Chesapeake Bay. Lightfoot and Mary had no children of their own to occupy that big house with them, but Jenny and Ruth, his two little sisters, lived there to help ease the burden on their ailing mother and to lessen Mary's anxiety about being without a child.[10]

Mary was helpful to her husband and to his family, yet she was disliked by some of the Michauxs. The old man resented her for several reasons: He believed she was too old for his son since she was seven to fifteen years older than he; her past was obscure except for the rumor that she had been a prostitute and he thought she had a mean nature. Reacting to this combination of reasons, he hardly spoke to her when she went to his store to visit or to shop. His reaction raises the question of whether the father disliked her because she reminded him of his wife in personality, although not enough is known about May Blanche to address this point adequately. She might have appealed to Lightfoot for the same reason that his father might have disliked her, because of a flawed, highstrung personality. Lightfoot knew Mary was mean-natured. Early in their marriage, he had given a woman neighbor a ride home from town. Mary was livid when she saw this and asked why he had not let her get home the same way she had gotten to town. Then she rushed outside and in a rage chopped up the axle of the automobile. From that day on, her husband never offered another woman a ride in his car.[11]

Their marital relationship bore signs of discord. In view of the circumstances of their coming together, it is doubtful that the Lightfoot Michauxs ever could develop an intimate relationship such as is often born of an initially passionate attraction. Their marriage developed out of an arranged courtship that was convenient for both. Lightfoot, like so many aspiring black men before him, had taken a light-colored, white-looking woman to be his wife, according himself more "status" in the black community, at least. This aspiring man of good reputation that she agreed to marry gave Mary an image of respectability, a good address, and comfortable living conditions. An unwritten feature of the "contract" was that Lightfoot did not need a continuously intimate and physically passionate attachment, if Mary did. His primary passion was the ardent pursuit of business interests. He cared for Mary but could contentedly leave her days and weeks on end to attend to business. So the marriage settled down, and he pursued the excitement of managing and building his business.

Then World War I erupted in Europe in 1914. It had a long reach and great impact on millions around the world. One of its interesting consequences concerned social and economic effects on the Negro in the United States. Black Americans supported their country sometimes sacrificially and enthusiastically during the war by volunteering for the Army and buying Liberty Bonds. Hundreds of thousands who migrated from the deep South to the North and from rural to urban areas to work in factories and plants also contributed to the war effort. Millions stayed home on the farm and in food related industries, and an unpublished story is that of the Negro's contribution to the United States program to produce and conserve food.[12]

Lightfoot did not go off to fight in the war. He stayed home and made profits from the war. He obtained government contracts to furnish food provisions for supply vessels which shipped American troops from the Newport News harbor to Europe. Shipments were so large and orders so frequent that he had to rent storage cabinets, with a 2 million pound capacity, right on the boat harbor. This enterprising businessman took advantage of every opportunity to make money, and he even schemed to boost profits. He had, for example, "green peas" in winter. They definitely were out of season in those days before advanced food processing, so he devised a process "to make dried peas look green." Dried peas sold for ten cents per pound and the price of green ones was double that. This kind of behavior, influenced by a prevailing business ethic which held that profit was the reliable index of progress and that rapid progress was most desirable, surfaced many times throughout his business life. According to this standard Lightfoot was progressing. Based on a steady inflow of government invoices and payment which mounted into thousands of dollars his profits were spiraling, and he invested fresh capital in branch stores. He opened these in nearby Norfolk and in the Petersburg-Hopewell area. The former was a shipping port and both had military installations where foodstuffs were sorely needed.

Business was exceedingly bullish in Hopewell, and Lightfoot had virtually an untapped market to himself. Reasons for this were obvious. Dupont had opened a guncotton plant there in 1915 and a phenomenal population increase of some 40,000 people followed. Local merchants in that small agricultural town were not adept at cornering such large markets. By the time they caught on, clever migrant merchants, like Lightfoot, already securely held lucrative business with large numbers of workers from the plant and with nearby Camp Lee.[13] Lightfoot spent most of his time in Hopewell and commuted to Newport News on weekends to bank money and to consult with the manager of that store. So when Mary, tired of contending with separation and loneliness, moved to Hopewell in 1917, he closed down operations in Newport News and Norfolk, moving the equipment and supplies into his father's thriving store.

While they prospered materially and Lightfoot preoccupied himself with business matters, in her loneliness, Mary's anxieties about their spiritual state heightened. It was her moralistic judgement that Hopewell's boomtown atmosphere was potentially corrupting. She tried to neutralize that potential by attending religious services as often as possible, reading the Bible and praying throughout the day, and evangelizing to all with whom she came in contact. Whereas in Lightfoot's more romantic opinion, Hopewell was "a wild and wooly place [where] nobody cared a hallelujah for Sunday worship"; so in the excitement, near hedonism prevailed. Lightfoot was intoxicated by flourishing business pursuits so regular church worship no longer held allure. There were a few places to worship, like the YMCA chapel, although it was empty while the adjoining beer parlor and gambling hall were crowded. Mary was not satisfied with whatever churches were in the town. She pestered her husband to build a church in which she could conduct services to her liking. So he built a small, white frame structure on land donated for that purpose by the Dupont Company. This experimental church was interracial, nondenominational, and evangelical. It was aptly called "Everybody's Mission." The church was an instant success. Hopewellians crowded into nightly services which were directed by visiting elders and Mrs. Michaux.

At the insistence of his wife, Lightfoot, who had lost his early interest in attending church, went to Sunday services. One day Brother Diaz, a Filipino evangelist who was an elder there, confronted him. "Brother Michaux," he said, "the Lord had you build the church, and you try to get everybody else to preach. But He wants you to do the job." It stunned Michaux that anyone could envision a minister being locked inside him, a compulsively ambitious, and, at times, unethical businessman. Religion and business were traditionally held to be antithetical, at least in theory, and his experience with religion was rooted in conventional Protestant denominations. Yet, Lightfoot, who was mission-oriented, could not shrug off the Filipino's chiding remark and Mary kept the notion constantly before her husband, inviting him to pray with her at home nightly. Following one soul-and-body-wearying session in 1917, Lightfoot received the "call" to preach.

There was no accompanying fanfare, no razzle-dazzle, no earth-shaking experience. There was only a commanding statement that struck him as he read John 4:35-36 in the Bible. He read the passage over and over: "Say not ye, there are yet four months, and then cometh the harvest? Behold I say unto you, lift up your eyes, and look on the fields; for they are white already to harvest. And he that reapest receiveth wages, and gathereth fruit unto life eternal; that both he that soweth and he that reapeth may rejoice together." He must have stared at the pages for a while, then prayed and talked with his wife. But he probably never articulated to anyone exactly what message he found in that scripture. Looking from a business orientation it is conceivable that the scripture, with its emphasis on how those who labor to reap the harvest are rewarded with wages, suggested to Michaux a relationship between business and religion. Perhaps he discovered in those verses that he did not have to abandon business to pursue a career in the ministry, and, in fact, might expand his business interests by entering the ministry. That next Sunday, in the little white church, Lightfoot announced to those assembled that he had received the "call" and that he would preach.[14]

Although historically formal training was not required of black preachers, by 1917 black professional and business folk expected their ministers to attend seminary. When he heard the news, Lightfoot's father assumed his son would attend the black Virginia-Baptist-supported Lynchburg Seminary and College since the family was Baptist. So he offered to pay for the schooling. But Mary went into a rage of opposition, saying she did not want Lightfoot to receive Baptist training because she thought Baptist preachers were unholy since several had made passes at her. Defiantly, she declared, "God will teach him what he needs to know." Lightfoot's father then suggested, during this family confrontation, that he should not preach if he did not attend seminary. Mary screechingly retorted, "If he doesn't preach, I will!" The confrontation ended. The family would be disgraced with a woman preacher but merely embarrassed before the community with an untrained son, so the senior Michaux pressed the issue no further.[15]

Mary took over and steered her husband back to the Church of Christ (Holiness) which they had attended in Newport News before going to Hopewell. Both were impressed with teachings of founder Bishop C. P. Jones. Prior to 1894 Bishop Jones was a Baptist preacher in Selma, Alabama, and Jackson, Mississippi. He said he left the Baptist Church to seek a faith that would make him a "friend of God" rather than a detractor. Jones alluded to the need that black folk, suffering under Jim Crow and attendant persecutions and poverty, had for God to be operative in their lives. He observed the Holiness movement which was popular among southern whites late in the nineteenth century. Seeing that it encouraged excitable religious experiences of conversion, Jones concluded that Holiness, rather than singing the blues, could provide black folk with continuous solace despite their plight. It was to this end that he then joined with C. H. Mason to establish the Church of God in Christ. He split from Mason's group and established his independent Church of Christ (Holiness) U.S.A.[16]

With her excitable disposition and interest in the teachings of Bishop Jones, no one was surprised that Mary influenced Lightfoot to become affiliated with that black, southern based Holiness convention. Details of his preparation, licensing, and ordination are unknown; however, acquaintances generally were aware that Lightfoot received counsel from Elder W. C. Handy, a seasoned Church of Christ preacher. Handy, who lived nearby, advised the fledgling elder on scriptural interpretation, pastoral duties, and church doctrine and practices. By mid-1918, Lightfoot was a licensed and ordained evangelist, with the right to pastor and "Everybody's Mission" became a Church of Christ affiliate.[17]

Now he was a businessman and a preacher. Under his careful supervision, the business continued to flourish and the church membership increased. Elder Michaux was "sitting on top of the world," relishing bountiful fruits from his labors in both the secular and spiritual realms.

Early on the morning of November 11, 1918, Allied Nations and Central Powers signed the armistice to end World War I. There was great rejoicing and much psychological relief everywhere. After celebration, men and women considered how they and their families would be affected. In some localities, such as in Hopewell, the effects of the terminated war were almost crashingly immediate. Wartime industries quickly dismantled, and business booms collapsed. The Dupont plant began shutting down operations in the same month that the armistice was announced. When it closed on January 1, 1919, twenty thousand men in Hopewell were left without jobs. Within another three months, the town's population decreased from over forty thousand to less than four thousand.[18] Like thousands of others, Lightfoot was troubled. His business had caved in and nearly all of his members had moved away. He sat surveying the wreckage wondering what he should do. He thought about home—Newport News.

That city had grown rapidly during the war. Industries had expanded. The population was approaching one hundred thousand. There was a building boom and real estate values had doubled since 1914. Relative prosperity still abounded. Jobs were available in the shipyard, on the C & O Railroad, and in the homes and stores which thrived because of these two industries.[19] Lightfoot thought it was a likely place for him to get a fresh start. After his own careful consideration, he talked it over with his wife and father. They agreed that he should return to Newport News at once and go into business with his father.[20]

Mary, who felt too lonely to stay at home away from the store as the senior Michaux and others preferred her to, was a daily irritant to all that worked there. The woman who had been their secretary during that time vividly recounted a scene which was typical of Mary's disruptive behavior in the store:

> She and I was talking. Awww we was just talking about each other. Then I wasn't saved sho' nuf. And . . . I said to her . . . Mrs. Michaux, you know one thing? People hear you up there in the pulpit almost preaching would think you was a heavenly gift, handed down from heaven. I said: You ain't nothing but a unknown devil. Awww she was combing her hair, and she had beautiful hair. Oh she jumped up to run out; he [her husband] said, "No, No, No! Come back here!" "Did you hear what Miss——— said to me?" He said, "You and Miss ———talking; when ya'll get through talking, I'll talk." And you know what his talk was? He reached right up on the desk and got the Bible, and he read the scriptures, and he got down and prayed. He asked her to pray. She said a little something short. He didn't ask me because he knew I wasn't saved then. He prayed. He made us shake hands. He said, "Miss ———, you come back to work tomorrow morning." The scriptures that he read—ooh they were so sweet! That's the way he settled it. She got so mad because he didn't say something [to correct me].[21]

There seemed to be no end to complaints about Mary from family and employees. If he wanted to lure her away from the store, Lightfoot had to leave. Added to his anxieties regarding Mary's petulance was his intense concern about his ministry. He decided to leave the business with his father and to organize a local Church of Christ (Holiness) mission. That would take care of both concerns, and he and Mary would subsist on savings and income from church offerings.

He fasted and prayed until confident that leaving the business to build a church was the proper course. His conviction came from a vision in which God showed him a field, ripe for harvest with 150 souls that would become members during revival. With much optimism on a September day in 1919, Lightfoot pitched a tent on the corner of Jefferson Avenue and Nineteenth Street, in the heart of the black community. There he and his wife conducted three months of high spirited, gospel festivity. From September to December, he preached, she led singing, and the congregation testified. Many curious townspeople went out to the tent to hear the home-boy preach. Domestics and teachers, professors from the local schools, doctors, lawyers, and their families, shipyard and C & O laborers, black and white merchants, and shopkeepers crowded in—many simply to observe the excitement and others in search of a meaningful religious experience. Those who joined the Michauxs found no mourners' bench in that revival. No one asked converts for an accounting of their conversion story or even suggested that a momentous "dungeon-shaking" conversion had to occur before one could join that group. To join one had only to give Michaux his/her hand, give God his/her heart, and promise to live above sin and condemnation while attending church regularly. At least 150 townsfolk joined during that three month period, verifying for Lightfoot that God was leading and directing him.[22]

These members were black, young adults, between nineteen and thirty, from the struggling masses who still held hope. Some had recently migrated to Newport News from the various southern states and from other areas of Virginia, such as Hopewell and the eastern shore, while others were born in and around the Tidewater. Most of the men were employed, either in the shipyard, on the C & O Railroad, in dock yards, or in the seafood industry.[23] The women worked mainly as domestics and in the seafood packing houses. A few members found other types of employment. For example, one was a jailer-sheriff, several were self-employed as carpenters, mechanics, barbers and beauticians, operators of boarding houses, and there were housewives (one was the wife of a local physician), and retired people.

For the most part Michaux's members were poor, propertyless, and without much formal schooling. Some had not attended school. A few had completed fourth or fifth grade and were functionally literate. The lucky ones, who had learned basics in reading, writing, arithmetic, and history, occasionally told spellbinding stories of how difficult those accomplishments had been to come by. In testimonies or during family gatherings, they talked about obstacles that they had to overcome to stay in school for those few years with one dress, no shoes, one pair of trousers, no transportation to schools miles away, and parents who did not understand the value of education or who thought they needed their children's help with chores at home or to earn an income more than the children needed an education. Because attending school so often was inconvenient they did not complete fourth or fifth grade until reaching the ages of twelve and fourteen. It was easy to drop out and almost as easy not even to ever enroll, although many hearts ached with longing to be well educated and some just to be able to read and write.[24] Michaux was comfortable at the helm of this group which he had awed, with the gospel and his personal successes, into taking a "stand for the Lord." His own intellect equalled and far excelled that of most of the members, he already had built and abandoned a lucrative business, and now was heeding God's Will by becoming pastor to these "special people"—God's remnant of the saints. This posture among them posed no threat to his self-image, indeed it enhanced it, as one of "superior" stock "called" to lead a "special people."

He expected the first months to be financially lean for the new church venture because he fully understood a little publicized fact about black church finance: money is scarce. Journalists and scholars have been correct in their observations which inspired E. Franklin Frazier to write that historically "Negroes pool[ed] their meager economic resources . . . [to] buy buildings and the land on which they stood."[25] But they never ask such administrative questions as: What proportion of their earnings is given to the church? With what consistency is it given? How long does it take to pay off church mortgages? And, at what rate are these mortgages refinanced? Michaux knew most black church folk regularly gave nickels, dimes, and quarters at that time with an occasional half dollar or dollar. He had not expected finances to be so scarce, though, as to keep them in the tent for three months but he was not surprised that after paying expenses, there was not enough money left to rent more comfortable quarters. Therefore, in the cold months of November and December, the Elder still was holding services under the patched-up tent, and to take the chill out of the air he fired-up a pot-bellied stove. Toward the end of December, there was finally enough money to move the church into a rented storefront one block east of the tent on Nineteenth Street and Ivy Avenue.

With electrifying excitement of the tent meeting behind, Light-foot settled down to the serious business of shaping his beguiled converts into models of Christian piety. These pliable ones eagerly gathered around him daily, at noon for prayer and in the evening for worship. Either seated at the head of the table or standing in the pulpit, Lightfoot generously interpreted biblical scriptures in order to give authority to his instructions. He carefully explained church doctrines, pointing out that rituals of baptism by immersion, of Holy Communion, and of foot-washing, like practices of tithing and giving offerings, were authorized in the Bible.

Patterns of moral behavior and cleanliness to which he expected conformity generally were imposed upon devout churchgoers. These two primary concerns extended from conditions under which black folk had existed as slaves. In slavery they lacked the legal protection and recognition of marriage, and spartan supplies of clothing, living facilities, and other articles issued by slave masters did not promote high standards of social and moral behavior. W. E. B. Du Bois indicates, in the turn-of-the-century study, *The Negro Church*, that institution's continued preoccupation with those concerns, for most Negroes still lived and labored under conditions of virtual slavery.[26] Michaux was a product of this black church, middle-class, "Lifting as you climb" orientation. The Holiness influence preened his bent. The Elder's requirements, then, that women not be consciously flashy or sexually provocative in dress and make-up and that no member lie or steal, curse, smoke, or drink, gamble or dance were not unduly harsh strictures for holy black people. It was reasonable, likewise, for Michaux to require members to be clean and well-groomed, and he taught them "cleanliness is next to Godliness." He tried to improve grooming habits among members by making special mention of those who always were clean and attractively dressed on their jobs and in church. Hoping to encourage all to be attractive, he sometimes complimented women who kept their hair neat (straightened) and who otherwise were tidy, not excluding those with tasteful make-up and earrings. In those early days, earrings were not banned; some women married in them, and one member wore them throughout her lifetime. When women who joined the church felt the need to rid themselves of obvious vanity and criticized earrings as sinful, not wearing them became standard with rare exception.

Probably school-aged children suffered most under weight of church strictures. They could not participate in May Day exercises or perform in school plays and programs. These little children were required by the church to remain apart from "worldly" influences and activities as much as possible. Michaux even discussed the possibility of the church's organizing its own school so the children could be educated without having to mingle with the "world." He had historical and contemporary models throughout the black church, including Pentecostal and Holiness groups, from which to draw, without necessity of mentioning other parochial schools that abounded. In nearby Belleville, Virginia, for example, Bishop William S. Crowdy had organized an industrial school for his Church of God and Saints of Christ, the Holiness assembly he founded in 1896.

It was less easy for Michaux to obtain conformity to some other standards which he or the denomination expressly imposed, such as dissolving common-law marriages. People engaged in that practice were protected by social sanctions of family privacy. If members did not admit to this practice, unless someone who knew them intimately became informer, common-law marriages went undetected in the church. So when the Elder discovered members living in common-law marriages, he spent a great deal of time teaching against the sin of adultery. He urged these members to leave the mate, or to leave the church if they did not marry legally.

Elder Michaux guarded members jealously. He made follow-up inquiries on those who were absent from daily sessions to determine if they were sick or caring for the sick, working during service hours, or slack in church attendance. To help guard against the latter, he urged members not to associate with sinners because he said, "You cannot keep fellowship with sinners and not be overcome with sin."[27] He encouraged them to create bonds of friendship among themselves. He prayed in pastoral sessions that members be bound together with a love surpassing that of earthly family relationships. He urged them to nurture the "first love" that still existed among them. Most members were impressed by these teachings and devoutly adhered to them, severing many strong family bonds. Members sometimes confided to each other that a sister or brother with whom they had been "bosom pals" was hurt that the intimacy had died. The severing of close bonds with family was undoubtedly a bitter pill for members to swallow. They never imagined that the Elder might have been incapable of the intimate exchange within relationships such as many of them had experienced. Not understanding that depth of emotion and sharing, the Elder robbed them of fulfilling experience. The kind of commitment to church required by Michaux caused the devout to end previous family and other intimate associations with nonmembers rather than be put out of the church.

There were members who even sacrificed men and women they loved in order to keep the fellowship. This is illustrated in the actions of a nineteen year old woman who quit her "unsaved" boyfriend. Giving him up was painful because theirs was a passionate affair. In order not to risk the chance that this young man might talk her out of quitting him, the woman said she had married a man in the Church of Christ (Holiness). That did, indeed, end the affair. The Elder's labors to keep members were rewarded, for only a handful of those who joined ever left that assembly.

The zealous Mary Michaux, otherwise unoccupied, helped win more converts. She formed a Prayer Band of women to go with her into the community. They knocked on doors and asked if they could enter to have prayer, as well as to cook and clean for those whom they found sick. A number came and joined the church as a result of those visits and zealous invitations. So thoroughly did Mrs. Michaux throw herself into this missionary work that according to one Prayer Band member, "She wore herself out," and suffered a protracted illness. She was ill for several months and death seemed imminent. In lucid periods, when she asked to go to church, Lightfoot carried her up and down the stairs in his arms. Those tender scenes compelled members to fast and pray that the woman whom their leader loved would have her health restored. When she became well again, the Michauxs and congregation thanked the physician for his treatments and medications and praised God for the healing as befitted a Holiness people.[28]

From all obvious appearances, the Michauxs were busily building another mission for the Church of Christ (Holiness) group in Newport News. This is why Lightfoot's members were surprised when he returned from the convention of 1921 and announced that he had left the Church of Christ (Holiness) U.S.A. They had not realized that he was troubled before going to attend that convention over a concern that had been smoldering inside him for several months. When the convention met in Jackson, Mississippi, in the spring of 1921, Michaux notified the bishop that he was seceding. He did not make his reasons public, yet his leaving was no more unusual than C. P. Jones' bolt from the Baptist Church had been in 1898. Ministers leave denominational and other church groups with a high degree of frequency. The variety of reasons for secession and the new groups and denominations that resulted are outlined well in Neibuhr's *Social Sources of Denominationalism*. C. Eric Lincoln also addresses this issue with special reference to black churches in their emergence from segregated white denominations.[29]

Later back in Newport News, the Elder revealed his reason for leaving. The bishop wanted to assign him to another mission after he had struggled to make this one thrive. Michaux said he chose not to leave this congregation which he had called out. After the bishop told Michaux he would be moved at the convention, Lightfoot secretly began making plans to leave the Church of Christ (Holiness). Back on February 26, he had incorporated the Gospel Spreading Tabernacle Building Association. In March that corporation had purchased the "Building"—a three story structure built by Benson Phillips, a white contractor and acquaintance from Michaux's childhood. The "Building" was on Nineteenth Street and Jefferson Avenue, across the street from where the tent had been situated.[30] Technically all gears were set for him to strike out on his own prior to convention time, but his members were not aware of his plans. Yet, when Michaux informed them of his decision in the aftermath, they readily agreed to follow him. They named their new, independent religious venture the Church of God because the Elder said that is what holy assemblies are called in the Bible.

The group moved into its new "Building" and continued the routine which had worked well for Michaux in the Church of Christ (Holiness)—calling members to daily church attendance and to study and practice Christian piety. Mrs. Michaux and her Prayer Band continued to proselytize in the community while the Elder concentrated his attention on increasing the membership and developing the spiritual life of the church throughout the next few months. Busy as he was this was a lonely time for Michaux. His father had died earlier that year, and he also had abruptly severed relations with Bishop Jones, the man who had been his spiritual father for several years. He tried to escape the loneliness through busyness.

He devised a plan to build his new organization into an empire that would be unsurpassed by other small religious groups. Highly motivated as he was to excel no one should have thought Michaux was single-mindedly preoccupied with building this lone assembly, nor should anyone have been surprised when he launched a new venture. Without fanfare, but as part of a long-range plan, he took the Gospel to the adjacent town of Hampton in the spring of 1922. The Church of Christ (Holiness) and other small religious bodies had a chain of churches, so could he. After receiving a sprinkling of converts in that meeting, he established a church in Hampton.

Those members were left alone enough, while Michaux held services in Newport News, to have time to institute a "mother-leader" within that congregation. This woman, late in her middle years, had emerged as counselor and decision-maker to members in Hampton. Instead of sitting on a pew, she sat apart, in a special chair. When he discovered this, Michaux swiftly abolished her "position" and her special chair. He then ordered members in Hampton to attend church in Newport News several times a week so they could thoroughly familiarize themselves with the chain of authority. The leader of every congregation was the Elder. Only he counseled and rendered decisions. In the black church the preacher always was titular leader. Michaux was determined to be leader in fact as well. For effective control, he monopolized the reins of authority within his infant organization. Thereafter, the Newport News and Hampton assemblies operated as virtually one body.[31]

During the predawn of one October morning in 1922, Michaux set the Church of God on another course of evangelism, and for the first time, he exhibited his flair for the dramatic. This happened as he led the congregation through the streets of Newport News loudly singing hymns of praise and invitation. Residents along the way were infuriated when this marching and singing recurred on several consecutive mornings, so they petitioned the police to stop Michaux and his band from disturbing their peace. Policemen met the noisy church group on the street one morning around five o'clock and arrested them. When one white member heard about the arrest, he immediately went to the jail, asking to be exchanged for Michaux. The bailiff explained that because Michaux was the group's leader, he would have to await a hearing before he could be released. Meanwhile the undaunted and faithful marchers held a prayer meeting in jail. They prayed, sang, clapped their hands, and shouted while two members, the white brother and a black justice of the peace, Emmet Fowlkes, arranged bail for the entire group.

When the trial was held, annoyed residents took the witness stand to testify against Michaux. They told of being aroused from sleep with a startle by the marchers who were singing loudly in the streets before dawn. That singing faded out as the group marched on, but when sleepy residents dozed off, they were awakened again by loud singing as the marchers doubled back on their way to a prayer meeting in the "Building." The municipal judge ruled that Michaux was guilty of disturbing the peace, fined him twenty-five dollars, and ordered him to stop holding the early morning street services. Michaux said the court's order was in error because it conflicted with his directive from God to use the street service to remind citizens to begin each day with prayer and singing. He appealed to the Virginia State Supreme Court for a writ of error. Meanwhile, Michaux pleaded his need to carry out God's cause from the pulpit. The Supreme Court turned down the appeal, and rather than pay the fine, the Elder presented himself to serve a jail sentence. But the judge hesitated to imprison Michaux who by then was something of a martyr among his members. He ordered instead that Michaux's automobile be seized and sold to pay off the small fine. To emphasize his belief that he was being persecuted for carrying out God's order, Michaux refused to accept the balance of money from the sale of the car, but he stopped the early morning street services.[32]

From that time on, people in the community began to scoff at Michaux not only because of his annoying marches but also because he had begun casting himself in the style of a mystic. He repeatedly made two controversial claims from his pulpit: First, that he had searched the scriptures and found that "God's perfect number is seven." Therefore, his being born on the seventh day of November with a caul indicated that his birth was of divine significance. Second, God had sent little angels to play with him in the crib and before the fireplace as if to verify the revelation of factors surrounding his birth. Significantly, these spectral playmates vanished when others entered into their presence. These claims circulated in the community and though they impressed members, they caused many outsiders to think Michaux was a joke and given to fantasy.[33]

In 1922 Michaux was a thirty-eight year old mission oriented preacher. His strong sense of personal worth buttressed his dedication to mission. This combination of psychological dynamos was tapped and nurtured by his disparate parents. Successes in business and in the ministry reenforced a sense of personal worth and validated Michaux's belief that he was "called" to mission. Driven by a compulsion to fulfill that mission, yet uncrystallized within his mind, he felt the need to be free from encumbrances against the "goal." Consequently, he established his independence by seceding from the Church of Christ (Holiness) and founding the Church of God. He embarked upon a plan of action which merged religious, social, and economic interests that he pursued with dramatic flair. By 1922 patterns of his later ministry were discernible, including the ability to appeal to masses by articulating their most intimate feelings and concerns.

2

About My Father's Business

As specifics of his mission were unfolding within his own mind, Lightfoot tried to articulate them to his congregation. In those early days, he told members that his role as preacher was comparable to that of courageous, Old Testament prophets. He had not anticipated how misunderstood that statement would be nor how it would create a problematic area in his ministry. Michaux already had shared stories with the congregation about the significance of his having been born with the caul over his face and about the visitation of spectral beings as his playmates. Unfortunately for him these claims, together with historical fact and contemporary phenomenon, combined to distort the image he intended and made moot his interpretation of his prophetic role.

Prophecy is a universal phenomenon. Though it has been with mankind through the ages, we are yet to accept comfortably those who claim ability to prophesy. That word conjures up images of sorcerers and diviners who draw upon supernatural forces to make foreboding predictions. Prophets, therefore, usually are the butt of wonderment and suspicion except among their adherents. For the most part, people's knowledge of prophets traditionally was limited to biblical and other historic accounts dramatized in sermons. One authority on the Old Testament explains that "Even when there is . . . interest in 'biblical prophecy,' popular understanding is distorted by preachers who sometimes give the impression that the biblical prophet gazed into God's crystal ball and predicted the shape of things to come."[1] Such dramatic accounts were made more credible during the 1920s by the emergence of black, contemporary, self-styled, exotic, prophet-messiahs, examples being Daddy Grace and Father Divine. Folk in Newport News had heard from acquaintances up North and via the press of these men's claims to supernatural powers, working of miracles, of their bizarre prophecies and exotic antics. The popular conception of prophets and Michaux's poor timing that made the announcement of his prophetic role concurrent with the emergence of Grace and Divine cast him in the image of "jive." Local folk expected him to pour forth bizarre predictions and to "work miracles." But this was contrary to Michaux's self-image. He did not envision himself to be "jive," a seer, nor a miracle worker who could raise the dead and heal the sick.

His interpretation of his role evolved from a more classical explanation of prophets. Unlike many, he understood and was guided by the Hebrew, Nabi', meaning of prophet as a messenger, God's spokesperson, a communicator of the Divine Will. He learned from Old Testament history that prophets understood themselves to be sent by God to communicate divine word to the people. Their authority lay in the One Who sent them. As Michaux understood it,

> The purpose of God's speaking through his prophet was not to communicate information about a timetable of events for the distant future. . . . Prophets often made predictions, . . . but these predictions, some of which came true and some of which did not, had reference to the immediate future, which impinged upon the present. . . . The prophet was primarily concerned with the present. His [or her] task was to communicate God's message for now and to summon the people to respond today.[2]

Noah, Miriam, Huldah, Isaiah, Jeremiah, and Joel were persons who predicted ordinary happenings based on human nature influenced by history and contemporary social and cultural occurrences. Their predictions merely were instruments for calling hearers to obedience to God's plan of righteousness.

Michaux made a statement about his mission which indicated that this was his sense of prophecy. "I present to you," he said in a sermon, "that which you need to know. . . . God has a plan . . . as one of those to whom He has revealed it, . . . I am endeavoring to cause everybody I meet to see the plan of salvation—salvation from death."[3] He carried out that role in light of the "Great Commission" by trying to propagate the gospel to all the world before the millennium and made only three predictions that he publicly labeled prophecies.[4] Under the burden of this prophetic mission, Michaux traveled from city to city, calling sinners to repentance and eternal life. He used the media, organized churches, and utilized his talents for showmanship to spread the gospel.

Though primarily motivated by his sense of prophetic mission, the Elder's decision to take the gospel to other cities also was a practical administrative move. It helped him keep his migrating flock in the fold. Economic stresses were forcing members to leave Newport News and Hampton to search for jobs. With its multi-port operations and industries, the peninsula had stemmed first blows of post-World War I recession. By the middle 1920s, however, business declined and brought on excessive unemployment that generally was widespread among black folk, and the situation was desperate for several members of the Church of God. Aware of resultant anxiety and frustration within his congregation and of less than full collection pans, Michaux called members together and set up a social welfare program to tide them and the church over the crisis. He called the program the "Common Plan." It was patterned after Christian communal living as outlined in the New Testament. Those who worked helped provide for those who were unemployed, and the latter prepared meals, washed and ironed, and performed other chores around the church home in exchange.[5] Despite these efforts to blunt blows of the recession, several church families joined others in leaving the area and going North to find jobs. Local newspapers captured the urgency of the situation among black people as they reported that "Many Negroes . . . have left Newport News and

Hampton . . . and the end is not yet."[6] The Elder followed his members to keep them in the fold.

The first group left the area in 1924 to find employment in the Pennsylvania coal mines. Among these seven or eight families were two deacons, their wives and children. They settled close to the mines which the men worked, but the several families sometimes lived miles apart. Using whatever transportation available, they gathered in their homes to hold prayer sessions as often as possible during the week, and on Sundays they conducted street meetings in an effort to convert others as the Elder had instructed. In 1926, several families moved about thirty miles from Edenborn to work in another coal mine, and because distance prohibited them from gathering with other members, they invited neighbors and coworkers to worship in their homes. When Elder and Mrs. Michaux visited the migrants, they conducted services in the Edenborn Community Hall. Later, in 1930, Michaux decided to organize an assembly there because Edenborn, fifty miles northwest of Pittsburgh, was central to most of his mining membership.[7]

A second family left Newport News in 1924, looking for jobs in Baltimore. Michaux made visits there also to worship with that family, and again he held services in homes. After several more members went to Baltimore, he launched a tent meeting. It drew crowds of white as well as black people in the area, including klansmen. No small source of klansmen curiosity at first must have been whether Michaux was black or white. At any rate he gained their ear. Determining that he was black they noted the decor of red, white, and blue bunting around the preaching platform and choir stand and appreciated the patriotic display following the war. Once their attention was attracted, they stayed and listened to lively singing and powerful preaching. Michaux preached on contemporary topics that cut across racial and denominational lines and addressed moral and social conditions. He, for example, defended prohibition and promoted a Victorian morality. He denounced jazz, dancing, and smoking, castigated the heathenism of communism, prophesied that the Second Coming of Christ was imminent, countered arguments that rejected the Virgin Birth and those that supported theories of evolution, and emphasized the brotherhood of man. Klansmen, like others gathering nightly under the tent, were enchanted, and those from Essex, Maryland, just north of Baltimore, invited Michaux to preach in their local church. This invitation baffled the Elder, making him a little anxious, for he was fully aware of the resurgence of the klan presence with its anti-Negro violence.

Until the "red scare" crisis of 1919-20, the newly organized KKK, which was revived in 1915 under the leadership of southern Methodist Episcopal preacher William J. Simmons, had remained small, impoverished, and regional. Capitalizing on anxieties that produced the red scare and Americanization-Immigration-Restriction-Movement along with race riots and prohibition, the klan spread North and West. It had widespread appeal among white leadership of growing towns and cities, and by the mid-1920s, hundreds of kleagles and millions of klansmen, from all social and economic classes across the country, burgeoned forth. Like their nineteenth century counterparts, they resorted to violence, intimidating their targets with cross-burnings and infiltrating communities with a barrage of assorted, demeaning literature. Everything about the klan was designed to encourage proscription of Catholics, Jews, black Americans, and recent immigrants. According to one historian, the KKK was the "primary organized defender of white Anglo-Saxon Victorian Culture, which in practice included the continued supremacy of the white Protestant male." That conspiratorial element kept racial, political, and religious minorities under daily threats of violence.[8]

Despite their intimidating history, Michaux was determined to take the gospel even to the KKK in order to fulfill his mission. With his wife and two other black female members, he went to preach for the all-white, KKK-infested congregation. The service was well attended, and everyone was hospitable to the black guests. Afterwards, Michaux felt rewarded for having preached there because at least one klansman, apparently with impunity from the kleagle, and his family joined the Church of God and regularly attended services in Baltimore. Presumably, the family severed its relationship with the klan. Michaux and members trusted him to the extent that they believed he had, and did not articulate a concern that he might have been a "plant" to directly observe and report on the

Elder's activities.[9] Michaux was confident that God was using him
to make these incursions against white exclusiveness and discrimination in and around Baltimore, and he believed God would protect him, even if someone intended to do him harm. He was so
encouraged by these feats that after establishing the Baltimore assembly
at 314 North Gilmore Street, in the heart of the city's black population, he decided to go home to test one of Virginia's recently en-
acted segregation laws that threatened his racially desegregated
services in that state.

Virginia's state legislature, like many others across the country
during the 1920s, was under the influence of KKK and other white
supremacist groups. In 1926 it passed a statute which required racially
separate seating in all places of public entertainment or assemblage.[10]
Virtually alone, Michaux challenged the application of that law to
the church. Since no one protested against his having two or three
white members and occasional visitors from the local community,
he deliberately invited his more visibly numerous white parishioners
from Maryland to live and worship with the predominantly black
congregation in Virginia. Law enforcement agents arrested Michaux
and charged him with illegally holding integrated baptisms, allowing
white people to room and board in the church's home with black
members, and allowing white and black worshippers to sit together
in church services. He contested these charges, telling the judge that
his work was in obedience to the "Great Commission" from Jesus
for disciples to go to all the world and preach the gospel to every
creature. He further advised the court that laws of God supercede
those of the State, that Virginia's ungodly segregation laws "must
stop at the threshold of God's House." His bidding for God fell on
deaf ears. Ruling him guilty the municipal court judge ordered a fine.
Michaux unsuccessfully appealed to the state supreme court for
reversal of that decision. He paid the fine and continued to violate
the state law as he taught all members that they must rise above
such statutes to worship and fraternize with each other or go to
hell.[11] He reminded those concerned about his safety that in Maryland God had moved on the hearts of klansmen and compelled them to
come into the midst of predominantly black congregates to listen to
the gospel. He had not been physically violated then and did not

fear bodily harm now, he told them. When the municipal court judge ruled against him, Michaux was not surprised. Using a Bible quotation, he exclaimed: "A prophet is not without honor, save in his own country."[12] But the Elder was undaunted.

As hundreds, even unexpected ones like klansmen, crowded under tents to hear him preach and to enjoy the rest of the service, Michaux was increasingly sure of his mission as one of God's spokespersons. Being of that mind he got the idea that he could gain an unlimited hearing by going to Washington to preach. When he arrived in that city in 1928, he declared that "intuition" had inspired him to go there.[13] Washington was a likely place for him to take his ministry since eyes across the country and of nations abroad observed activities and news from the Capital. Michaux reasoned that a strong local assembly there could provide him with a base for a far-ranging pulpit. Awaiting his arrival was a likely population to tap.

There was within that city a colony of black migrants who were alienated, since the established residents consisted of pretentious, light-skinned Negroes, upper-class snobs and white racists. These apparently disoriented migrants made good prospects for an enterprising preacher. With his congregational base of support from Baltimore, he went right in and held a series of tent meetings on Sherman Avenue. Each night the tent was packed. Most of those who attended and joined the church had recently come to Washington. Based on his appeal among them, Michaux looked for a church site nearby and located a temporary one in a U Street storefront.[14]

The Elder just had started that church when he got the notion that a marvel in technology, radio broadcasting, would be the forum for his ministry. He already had experiences from which to draw: The first religious radio service was beamed from Pittsburgh in 1921 by the Reverend Edwin Van Etten, an Episcopal minister.[15] Michaux might have heard about that when he went to Edenborn in the Pittsburgh area. He later broadcasted from his church in Newport News over a portable station. His "intuition" about radio's potential for widespread evangelism, before that medium came fully of age, was of prophetic dimensions. The idea was seminal. It would develop further within Michaux's mind and eventually mature into a grand and complex design, engendering media-oriented evangelism in other places and generations.

Michaux's initial goal was modest, but its potential for expansion is discernible. His thinking was based on the belief that the decline in church attendance could be made more negligible in its effects by radio evangelism. His immediate interest was in getting the gospel to Washingtonians who stayed away from churches. Michaux summed up the thinking this way: He aspired to broadcast services "so [people] might have religion at home. Then they would have no excuse for not going to church. . . . They couldn't say they were tired or didn't have the right clothes. They could get God and His teaching right in their own Parlor."[16]

Inspired by "intuition," from 1928 to 1929, Michaux went to almost every radio station in Washington, trying to locate a program spot. He could not even get an appointment to meet with most program managers. His difficulty was partially a reflection of the Capital's racial cleavages. Race and other minority relations were tense, and black people were noticeably segregated and denied equitable participation in the mainstream of business and political activities. The former Washington historian, Constance McLaughlin Green, described malevolent effects of white, Anglo-Saxon Protestantism as "setting apart white from Negro, Gentile from Jew . . . clique from clique, and cave-dweller from upstart."[17] The tenacious Michaux, who battled against forces of segregation in Virginia and stirred hearts of avowed klansmen in Maryland, doggedly pursued station managers. He would not give up. Finally, he got an appointment with the owner of radio station WJSV, James S. Vance, to ask him for a spot. Vance was also printer of the KKK publication *Fellowship Forum*. Michaux might have been aware of Vance's KKK connections and so approached him on the strength of his previously rewarding experiences with that racially conservative organization. According to a local newspaper reporter, contemporary observers were amused that Michaux would entertain the idea "that a klan associate should sponsor a Negro's devotional enterprise. . . . But Michaux sold himself so thoroughly to Vance . . . that . . . [he] agreed to foot the expense of [the Elder's] broadcasting an hour a week from the storefront on U Street."[18]

The inclination to launch the radio program in 1929 was well-timed. That was the eve of radio's golden era which would come in the 1930s. The Great Depression, a time when people abandoned futile pursuit of the deceitful Mammon and sought other diversion, such as entertainment, partially accounts for radio's rapid ascendancy. Michaux's broadcast was in that windfall. He became almost instantly popular and within three years was broadcasting daily to millions of listeners across the United States.[19]

The radio broadcast is a good example of how Michaux set out to advance his prophetic mission by employing showman techniques. Although detractors seized upon that term to describe and criticize his ministry, he saw nothing negative about showmanship. He held a technical view of it, for to him showmanship was a tool for drawing crowds to preach to. From that perspective, he was not unlike today's biggest preacher-attractions such as Robert Schuller, Oral Roberts, Pat Robertson, Reverend Ike or Jerry Falwell. Several of Michaux's contemporaries were also preacher-showpersons; the revivalists Billy Sunday and Aimee Semple McPherson are two prime examples. Indeed, Michaux worked hard and long to design the kind of radio program which would catch and hold listeners' attention until he could preach to them.

Every broadcast signed on with the catchy, syncopated theme song, "Happy Am I," causing fans to call the Elder the "Happy Am I Preacher." That label was appropriate because the song reflected the evangelistic tone and apocalyptic philosophy that underscored Michaux's basic message. The verses alone captured the essence of that message.

> Sweetly I trust in my Redeemer as I go singing on my way,
> Daily I know that He is with me, keeping my soul from
> day to day;
> Sweetly I sing along the journey, helping the lost to
> know His way,
> Hoping to meet Him in the morning, in the eternal
> home above;
> Looking for Him most any moment, ready when Jesus
> shall appear,
> Keeping my lamps all trimmed and burning, feeling His
> coming now is near.

Each verse ended with "Happy Am I, yes, Happy Am I." Then with lyrics to the chorus, why "I am happy" was explained:

Happy Am I with my Redeemer, singing along
the home-ward way,
And telling the lost of His great love,
of His great mercy;
Happy Am I to know He's with me, keeping me
spotless day by day,
I'm happy along the way to heav'n above
Along the way.[20]

This simple, straightforward message to millions, caught in the throes of economic depression, hopeless destitution, and dejection, was that you can trust God to be with you as you travel through this perilous life, and Jesus, Who will return, will take the redeemed to a home of eternal bliss in heaven. Three themes, which reverberated throughout the Elder's sermons, were synthesized within this signature song: The first was that conditions in this world are hazardous to man's soul, and destruction is imminent. Second, if you accept God into your life, the Divine One will protect you through earthly trials and sorrows. Finally, with God in your life, you can be happy here and hereafter.

Day after day, Sunday following Sunday, Michaux preached that the world has become increasingly wicked since the days of Christ's Ascension, and it is now headed for the same destruction that God rained down upon the infamously, sinful Sodom and Gomorrah. With heavy reliance on Scripture, he emphasized this theme in a sermon that was typical of his preaching style. When Apostles asked Jesus what shall be signs of the end, Michaux said,

[He] told us of this day that you, who walk in His way, might know that *it is all about today.* "Jesus answered and said unto them, take heed that no man deceive you." (I'm going to tell you what the signs will be *now* but *after* I've told you, don't let any man deceive you.) "For many shall come in my name, saying, I am Christ; and shall deceive many. And ye shall hear of wars and rumors of wars. . . . Nations shall rise up against nations." (It's here.) "And kingdom against kingdom, and there shall be famines and pestilences and earthquakes in divers places." (These are the beginnings of sorrows.) "Then shall they deliver you up to be afflicted" (They are going to take you who sit here now with Me on this peaceful Mount of Olivet and they're going to afflict you.) "And shall kill you."

Pausing to emphasize persecution of Christians and the imminent danger in which the righteous always stand when among the wicked, Michaux pointed out,

(And that's what they did. Everyone of those Apostles were killed just as Jesus had spoken except one; that one was John the Beloved. They exiled him to the Isle of Patmos; they tried to destroy him with wild beasts. But God sent a raven to feed him because God wanted to reveal to him the things that He wanted the church to know. And whenever God is for you, nobody can be against you.)

Then the Elder returned to his main text, further explaining how Christians would be affected by the evil around them:

(And so my brother and my sister, it is stated here [in Matt. 24]) "Ye shall be hated of all nations for my name's sake, and then shall many be offended, and shall betray one another and shall hate one another. And many false prophets shall rise and shall deceive many. And because iniquity shall abound the love of many shall wax cold."

Michaux had particular reference to his own prophetic ministry when he quoted this passage of Scripture, "And this Gospel which I have taught you must be preached in all the world for a witness unto all nations, and then shall the end come."[21]

In another radio sermon, he enumerated sorrows and crises from the Great Depression, implying their fulfillment of Scriptures in the "last days."

Thyroid glands of the nation's economic system, which is the "banks," had overworked itself [sic] until their assets were no more liquid than frozen custard. Stocks and bonds of . . . many industries that had paid handsome dividends had become worthless. Millions of dollars worth of mortgages on the finest kind of property had lost their value. The foreclosure on homes of many a poor working man and his family whose equity in the home represented his life's saving was in process.
   Great railroads were hauling empty passenger coaches and freight cars. . . . Products of farmers rotted in the fields because of no market. Young students were turned out of universities and colleges . . . because no money came from their parents to pay tuition. . . . Mental pressure was too great; many committed suicide.

> . . . Men began to leave their homes and families seeking work in
> other towns. . . . Finding no work they began to turn on society,
> becoming gangsters and racketeers. Bootlegging had become the chief
> business of the people of this nation. . . . Many bankers and business-
> men, politicians, officers of the law, racketeers, and gangsters joined
> hands, trying to survive the depression by bathing the nation's sorrows
> in poison liquor.[22]

Previously he had compared President Roosevelt's handling of
the depression crisis to Moses' leading the Israelites out of the desert.
It was in 1934 when Michaux remarked,

> Franklin D. Roosevelt, . . . is a modern Moses leading the American
> people out of the wilderness of despair and economic chaos. Leaders of
> government are ordained of God, and the righteous are enjoined to
> regard them as such and to support them. . . . If we [the nation of
> people] reject the New Deal offered us by God through . . . Roosevelt,
> there is nothing left for us but chaos.[23]

According to the Elder, a people could wreak havoc upon themselves by rebelling against leadership anointed by God. The inference
was no matter how much the nation suffered during the Great Depression its troubles would be intensified if the New Deal was rejected because it was "authored" by God.

Michaux would have his listeners conclude from these sermons
that man cannot escape troubles and destruction. Either the earth
will be destroyed eventually or the millennium will occur. Meanwhile man will suffer war, pestilences, sorrows, and even saints will
have trials and tribulations. The Great Depression and biblical
history provided evidence for this conclusion, the Elder would have
his listeners believe.

Amidst the gloom and doom, however, Michaux offered those in
radioland a formula of hope for those who would heed God's Word
and be redeemed. "God planned," he instructed in one sermon,
"before the world was created, that a certain number of people,
regardless of anything that happens, should be holy and without
blame before Him in love." Making this a personal message to individual listeners, he continued,

God had to have somebody, and according to his foreknowledge of
you and me as to what we would do and how we would be. He made
a choice of a number of people for every age who would lift up
righteousness. . . . So it says here, [that He] predestinated us unto
the adoption of children by Jesus Christ to Himself.[24]

Michaux's counsel was that only the elect can live up to the teachings
of Jesus Christ and standards of holiness. In order to live holily,
we must be born again, that is, we must be baptized with the Holy
Spirit. We must be adopted into the family of God that the Elder said
has several groupings of children:

Angels [who] are created sons of God . . . are spirit beings. . . .
[Another] created son was Adam [a] human being. . . . The begotten
son, both human and divine [was] Christ; the Lord has adopted
sons, . . . Those who walk not after the flesh . . . become sons of
God by adoption [and] are made equal with Christ and the angels.[25]

Michaux took this male-slanted, Fundamentalist-type gospel and
applied it to contemporary conditions, giving his sermons a "New
Thought" flavor. He preached about human relationships and spoke
of how people could live harmoniously and charitably with each
other by accepting Christ into their lives. After all, he said, "sin is
trespassing the right of your fellowman. God ordained that we live
together in love and be happy in this beautiful, created world. But
we became alienated from God, . . . from the commonwealth of
Heaven [by the Fall of Adam and Eve]."[26] He previously had preached
in an earlier sermon, taking his text from I Cor. 13,

Though I speak with tongues of men and of angels and have not
charity, I am become as sounding brass and tinkling cymbals. . . .
[Leaders of nations] are ministers of God, . . . [and when] divinely
directed . . . [like Franklin Roosevelt, will show] unlimited charity
toward the people . . . considering human rights far above property
rights in the face of all opposition thrown up by those who desired
to be the favored few.[27]

These sermons that addressed social relations articulated human
needs and hurts to which national leaders should be sensitive. More

pertinently, Michaux practiced a religious ethic that involved itself in the secular realm to address spiritual and material needs. He defined religion as "an active, daily effort to improve life." He explained that his assembly "entered the sacred domain of private enterprise in order to help people."[28] He believed the Christian church and Christians should lead the way in showing the world how to be loving, peaceful, cooperative, just, and charitable. The Christian church should be a watch-dog over government and its leaders. The result would be a more equitable kingdom on earth, for social institutions, laws, and social practices would be aligned with Christian principles. Racial segregation, discrimination, and violence, economic and political exploitation, inequities of class, bigotry, inhumanity, poverty would disappear. This sentiment formed a central hope for victims of racism and capitalistic exploitation. Because of his experiences of being black in a white dominated society, questing for the elusive "American Dream," Michaux's insertion of "New Thought" philosophy into his Fundamentalist-type gospel was inevitable.

He believed in social and moral improvement, but his understanding did not extend to institutional reform, per se. As a Christian missionary, he was committed to principles of the conversion of individuals from sin to holiness. Synonymous with that conversion, within his mind, were commitment and devotion to Christian thought and practice. Committed Christians in aggregate would yield a citizenry responsive to eradicating evil and human needs and sufferings. A consequence would be a Christian democracy as opposed to what he then saw as a nation of people merely professing democracy and Christianity.

Because Michaux's view of what society could be was an ideality, he pointed out how individuals within an imperfect world could benefit from spiritual rebirth. Those who are reborn will be joint-heirs, with Christ, throughout eternity, to the kingdom of Heaven. "Notice, my precious ones," he said, "that there are two resurrections—one of the Holy and the other of the sinner [, following the millennium]. . . . Blessed and holy is he that hath part in the first resurrection. . . . [The holy will] meet Jesus when He shall return. He's coming back to meet [and catch up in the air] those He taught how to be like Him." With this promise, the reborn should be happiest of all earthly creatures because they have the promise of a good life here and hereafter. Either you will have a foretaste of heaven here, he stressed, or "you have small chance to live hereafter." Within this same vein, he would say, "I don't believe in nobody who goes around [professing to be] doing God's will if they are hard up. The way of the transgressor is hard."[29] At the end of the millennium the kingdom of Heaven will descend to earth, and the saints will judge sinners, who, with Satan, will be cast into the lake of fire and brimstone to suffer forever.

While his eschatalogical dogma centered on a literal interpretation of the Bible, Michaux's ideas on the relationship of religion and society were more eclectic. They were strangely similar to "New Thought" and "Social Gospel" concepts expressed by Theodore Parker and later more practically applied by Walter Rauschenbusch, a Baptist preacher who labored among the poor around the turn of the century. Espousing a message of Christian social reform, he expounded on this theme: "The essential purpose of Christianity was to transform human society into the kingdom of God by regenerating all human relations and reconstituting them in accordance with the will of God."[30] Based on this philosophy and his attempts to apply it, Rauschenbusch became leader of the Social Gospel movement in this country. It is conceivable that Michaux was familiar with concepts from this movement, for he hired tutors to teach him classical and theological materials when he became famous. For years a succession of tutors shuttled in and out of his home at 1712 R Street, NW. They read to and had him recite content back to them until he felt comfortable to use the newly acquired knowledge.[31] Michaux's perception of Social Gospel ideas would have been that of one standing outside the mainstream of the society and virtually powerless to influence reform of the institutional system. Therefore, his was a gospel of social consciousness closely linked with personal salvation/redemption that in aggregation could lead to a more perfect society, while Rauschenbusch emphasized social redemption that could lead to collective salvation.

A people confused and stunned by the Great Depression and frustrated by the still ongoing controversy between science and religion could find much that was appealing in Michaux's sermons. They had a conventional tone and gave simple explanations to complex social issues and problems which then preoccupied the nation's attention. It was easy to conclude from these sermons that the great economic crisis and human suffering were results of rampant sin among business leaders and government ministers. The easy solution was to eradicate sin, to "war on the devil." The nation could wage a moral crusade and save the democracy, or failing that individuals could seek conversion to righteousness so that they would be allied with God. God would provide an island of tranquility amid chaos and supply all needs and many wants. Some who heard this message of seeming free-will thought it contradictory to the Elder's doctrine of predestination. If he recognized the contradiction, Michaux was undeterred, in offering his interpretation of the Plan of Salvation and of social and moral improvement based on free-will acceptance of salvation.

Undoubtedly many listeners were more entertained by Michaux's style of preaching than were inspired by his gospel message. Although he had no formal theological training, the radio evangelist had diligently studied the Bible and had developed an appealing preaching manner. He skillfully used the Bible, calling out scriptures and quoting from them. That was impressive at a time when preachers frequently were accused of not preaching from the Bible. One of the Elder's first members, in fact, said she was "not used to people preaching and calling Scriptures." The first time she heard his Bible-centered gospel, she joined the church.[32] Also making observation on this technique, a reporter asked, "Does the Elder know his Bible?" Then he answered, "Rather literally backwards and forwards. Sometimes he quotes passages ten to twelve times in a half-hour period, giving the chapter and exact verse number in most instances."[33] Michaux's procedure was to call for a Scripture, have a deacon read it, then the Elder would repeat and explain as it was read. He said this was a method adopted by him so that whatever was said could be checked against the Scriptures.[34] That technique is illustrated everywhere in his sermons, and this excerpt is typical.

In Matthew, the 24th chapter reading the 8th verse, the Scripture says, "These are the beginning of sorrows." Read! "All these are the beginning of sorrows." The things that are now upon the earth such as nation upon nation and kingdom upon kingdom are the beginning of sorrows that Jesus declared should come upon the earth preceding the end of the world.

In Matthew the 24th chapter and the 22nd verse, you'll find the text
which reads, . . . "And except those days should be shortened."
Except the days should be shortened, "There should be no flesh
saved." We are now heading for utter destruction unless the nation
prays.[35]

The interaction between reader and preacher created a liveliness
suggested in this excerpt.

Find in your Bible in Matthew, 27th chapter, reading from the 50th
to 53rd verses, inclusive and listen to what it says. . . . Read! "And
the earth did quake, and the rocks rent." There was an earthquake
and the rocks burst apart. "And the graves were opened; and many
bodies of the Saints . . . " Who was that? "And many bodies of the
Saints . . . " How about sinners? "And many bodies of the Saints . . . "
How about Christians? "And many bodies of the Saints." What did
they do? "And many bodies of the Saints which slept arose." No
matter what I ask, it won't change God's words.

In Psalms 116, reading the 15th verse, you'll find these words for
your information; find it in your Bible! "Precious in the sight of the
Lord is the death of His Saints." It didn't say a word about the death
of a Christian.[36]

Michaux's preaching was stirring but not vehement. Audiences
interacted with him enthusiastically and in a fashion reminiscent of
the call and response so noticeable in black Baptist churches. Michaux's
wife and others shouted throughout his sermons, "Yeah!" "Amen!"
"That's right, Elder!" "Preach!" "Yeah, praise the Lord!" He plied
audiences with rhetorical questions that would catch attention and
interest, such as "Do you hear and understand that?" Then he would
recoil with this kind of answer, "God said it; I didn't."[37] Or he would
strike with "Listen!" "Notice!" He could be strikingly personal, as
if addressing each person individually, for example: "Just as surely
as you are sitting on your chair in here, in your home or wherever
you may be, it is coming to pass."[38] The Elder even sprinkled
"amens" throughout his own sermons, and at times confided to his
congregations, "You can always tell when the Holy Ghost and
Power come down. I got burnt this morning myself."[39] Following

such interaction, he always beseeched those in his audience to seek salvation with statements like: "Don't let anybody fool you. The Bible tells the story. See that your name is written on the Book of Life; you need to have it written there."

Sometimes listeners marveled at the way Michaux simplified points, explaining them by using familiar illustrations. In a sermon on "Why the Revised Standard Version of the Bible Cannot Be Accepted By A Christian," the Elder said he trembled over that version's deletion of the word "begotten" from John 3:16. That omission erroneously made Jesus God's only son, he said. Michaux explained instead that God has many sons—created sons (adams and angels), a begotten son (Jesus), and adopted sons (saints). He instructed listeners that

> An adopted son is made equal with a son which is born into a family, that is if he is legally adopted. And though I was not a created son like Adam, though I was not a begotten son like Jesus, I am an adopted son and I'm made equal with Christ and the angels.[40]

In a sermon on the millennium, Michaux showed how the world would be judged from records that are in Heaven of daily lives on earth. He related it to listeners' working experiences.

> Records are kept right here on the earth. If you work for a company of any size, they have your record. They know everyday that you work and every hour that you put in; they know the quality of the work done by you—it's on record. If man is that intelligent to want to judge his workers to find out if they are good or bad workers, what about God?[41]

Michaux also sprinkled sermons with catchy aphorisms to help him clarify a point. He would exclaim, for example, "God is a business God—He keeps records," or "God is the Father of people," or "You'll be a devil if you disobey Christ." Such imagery in aphorisms marks effective black preaching. A reporter unfamiliar with that characteristic of black sermons, however, reached back to the eighteenth century to find a comparison of Michaux in Benjamin Franklin.[42]

With its rasping quality, the Elder's voice was not that of an orator, but he compensated for that lack with technique. Preaching with his eyes closed most of the time, his face "took on a rapt expression as if he were . . . getting the holy word direct from God." One church publication described his preaching in this manner:

> [He] always had . . . a glimmer of a smile shining in the lineaments of his large brown face, yet always with a ghostly sadness haunting his intelligent features. Always distrait, as he is even in his most intense moments of exhortation, yet so keen and alert in mind that his very word is a hook-up with his immediate surroundings and the last word spoken.[43]

Michaux's preaching and then novel and peppy program contributed to his soaring popularity as a radio evangelist among blacks and whites, both socially prominent and socially disinherited. Therefore, when Vance sold his independent station to Columbia Broadcasting Systems in 1932, the Elder's broadcast was the only program retained by the new owners. Michaux credited Harry C. Butcher, then vice-president of CBS, with keeping him on and with giving him national airing.[44] By 1933, fifty-two stations beamed Michaux's program from coast to coast. Additionally, short wave took the broadcast to Europe, South Africa, and India, making Michaux "one of a handful of persons whose opinions ever had been aired over the international short wave."[45] It was a short step from the Elder's current international forum to his vision of spreading the gospel to all the world. He talked-up this aspiration to members and tried to make it theirs too. He believed the gospel would reach all people, then the End would come. In view of his record, Michaux was not unreasonable in believing he would be the instrument God would use toward that propagational goal. He already was broadcasting on four continents.

When they released statistics on the program in 1934, CBS officials estimated that 25 million Americans tuned in on Saturday nights, a prime time, and that over 2 million listened to the "Happy Am I" program daily. Thousands rained fan mail on the evangelist. From October 1933 to September 1934, he received over 1,000 pieces of mail per day, necessitating delivery in a special Post Office truck and employment of fifteen secretaries to sort and read.[46] Fans wrote

to Michaux from many parts of the United States and from over-
seas—from California, Kansas, Rhode Island, Ontario, and the
British Isles. Curious fans journeyed from Maryland, Virginia,
Tennessee, North Carolina, Pennsylvania, New York and Massa-
chusetts.[47] Hundreds similarly showed appreciation for the program
by going to Washington to observe a broadcasting session in the
new Church of God edifice on Georgia Avenue. They made pilgrim-
ages in heavily laden buses, on trains, and in automobiles. One man,
who went up from the South in 1933, said enthusiastically, "I just
wanted to know if it was a radio affair or whether it was real." He was
excited about the dramatic staging of the broadcast that featured a
forty-voice, white-robed choir, uniformed band, a little "Prayer Girl"
who, dressed in white, led the audience in praying the "Lord's Prayer," the
nattily dressed Elder and his golden-voiced wife, and often some
prominent personage. The program had a brisk pace, with rapid
movement from one type of performance to another. It would flow
from choral music to vocal solo, to prayer, to instrumental solo, to
readings of the Scripture, to more choral music, and then to a sermon.
Each performance was precisely timed. Michaux planned the variety
carefully not only for the sake of entertainment but also to keep his
unpredictable wife in close rein. Responding to the exciting radio
show the same man from the South marveled, "I have never seen anything like this. I am happy that I traveled 500 miles."[48] Hundreds of
others concurred with his sentiment, and many returned.

   Pleasure-seeking U.S. and foreign dignitaries from around the
Capital also stopped in to see Michaux's broadcast. Lord and Lady
Byng of England, a group of Oxford University scholars, the then-
Secretary of State and Mrs. Stimson and Mrs. Eleanor Roosevelt
were among the many. Other prominent ones, who did not attend
services, invariably tuned in, as did Mrs. Mamie Eisenhower. She
said, in later years, she frequently listened because Michaux "impressed her that he always had something good to say on any subject."[49]
Ethiopians, Czechs, and various other diplomats dropped in to witness a
broadcast.[50]

   Newsmen went to observe the radio services so they could interpret
Michaux to their readers. Their main point of analysis was the Elder's
popularity. Some reporters thought he owed his notability to the
"Happy Am I" song. It had caught on around the nation. "The
United States Marine Band had it arranged for its musical presenta-

tions and included on its nationally famous programs. . . . One could hear [people whistle the tune while] walking along the streets."[51] It reached Hollywood, and Eddie Cantor's staff put new lyrics to the tune and introduced it as original on Cantor's Works Progress Administration Kentucky Colonel radio show. Michaux recognized it as the tune of his theme song and protested. Cantor's writers admitted similarity and agreed to squelch their ditty.[52] Gauging his popularity, newsmen variously dubbed Michaux the "world's greatest radio evangelist," "radio evangelist extra-ordinary," "best known colored man in the United States today." Because he was so popular, white reporters thought to compare him to white evangelists. Several claimed they recognized in Michaux blended qualities of famous, colorful preachers, as, for example, Billy Sunday, Aimee Semple McPherson, Seth Parker, and Father Coughlin. One reporter enthused, "Elder Michaux goes Billy Sunday one better" though. But another correctly countered, "That really isn't accurate. There's not a trace of the 'sliding down a banister and hitting the saw-dust' sort of thing," for which Sunday was well-known, in Michaux's style. Yet another offered, "He possesses all that knack and happy faculty of his white contemporary, Billy Sunday, to hit the nail on the head every time in a picturesque broadside of vernacular, slang and popular allusion. But he is less vitriolic than Sunday, and always bubbling over with humor."[53]

The popular evangelist created a sensation wherever he went. He packed public auditoriums beyond capacity, always with racially mixed groups. An example was the special revival, at the Belasco Theatre in 1933, to welcome President Roosevelt to Washington. There was an overflow crowd. "Fire and police squads had to call for reserves to handle . . . [the swarm of people] during [that] meeting . . . and . . . [these officers requested] that no more songs be sung because . . . [they] fear[ed] that the swaying of the crowd in time to the singing would actually bring down the crowded balconies."[54] He attracted another huge and enthusiastic crowd when he held a revival in the Philadelphia Arena in 1934. That meeting, from which the church at Philadelphia was started, was hosted by a civic group headed by Major R. R. Wright, a prominent, black banker. Moreover, Michaux preached to packed audiences in both the Mosque and the City Auditorium in Richmond, Virginia, as well as to thousands in the Atlantic City Auditorium, the Mosque at Altoona, Pennsylvania, and in open-air and tent meetings, such as those at Hanover and Philadelphia, Pennsylvania.[55] But nowhere was attendance higher than at Annual Baptizings. Michaux engaged Griffith Stadium for these services. Billy Sunday took note of the stadium services during his declining days when he quipped, "Any man who had to hire a national baseball park, seating 35,000 to hold . . . meetings is the man to preach the gospel."[56] Scores of invitations flowed in, from church groups across the country during the 1930s, requesting that Michaux bring his Cross Choir and conduct revivals. At least one white group suggested that he pass for white and accept a call to its pulpit.[57]

Sensationalism surrounding the Elder did not go unnoticed by giant entertainment enterprises. Ignoring its potential loss of $3,000 per day in rent, the Madison Square Garden Corporation made an unprecedented move when it granted Michaux free use of the Garden to run a revival in 1934. That also was the first time a black group had been given access to the Garden. Paramount and Warner Brothers officials recognized a moneymaker and asked Michaux to collaborate with them in making a movie based on his radio broadcasts and other religious services. Refusing that offer he produced a film variously entitled "War on the Devil" or "Happy Am I." It was seen by thousands during the premiere viewing at Madison Square Garden. (A few years later, the Elder cooperated with Jack Goldberg to make the compilation film, "We've Come A Long, Long Way," in 1942.)[58] Following the Madison Square Garden appearance a New York booking agency offered Michaux $3,000 per week to appear in a daily show with his Cross Choir. According to critics this choir compared favorably to the famous Hall Johnson Choir that appeared in all-black movies, such as the 1930 allegory, "The Green Pastures." Michaux proudly showed that letter around but refused to sign a contract with the agency.[59]

After such recognition in the American entertainment field, few people were surprised in 1936 when Felix Crum, a representative of the British Broadcasting Corporation, contracted Michaux to broadcast occasionally to the British Empire. Englishmen had long-standing fascination with Negro culture, and Crum's response to the Elder was based on this fact. He invited Michaux, Crum wrote,

because he had been "enormously impressed . . . [by his] skill in
going from one song to another—particularly in the way [he] called
out questions to which the choir responded—and also the humor
and humaneness with which [he] did this." Beyond that, Crum expressed an interest in Michaux's broadcast that was reminiscent of
white folk who went "slumming" in Harlem during the 1920s, as he
laid out last minute details in his letter to the Elder:

> The chief thing is to make the listener in England feel that he is listen-
> ing—not to a service specially put on for him—but to a normal
> Negro gathering. . . . In a queer way a service of this kind, known
> to be specially arranged, loses authenticity. . . . I want my country-
> men at home to realize the power there is in a group singing with real
> religious spirit and fervour. You see, we have become far too genteel
> a race ever to let ourselves go—especially in religion! Only the Welch
> still have that grand abandon.

Then Crum requested that the choir sing "Lift Him Up," "Standing
in the Need of Prayer," and "We've Got the Devil on the Run" in
the first broadcast that fall.[60]

By this time, Michaux was comfortable and confident in his role
as a spokesman for God. During the summer of 1936, he declared,
"I don't say I am the only prophet, but if any other comes along in
this age and doesn't speak in accord with what I speak, he is a false
prophet."[61] But when he seemed most comfortable in his "posture,"
props were knocked out from under him. A chain of apparently
unrelated events occurred, and these may have been consequential
to the Elder's plummet from the international radio scene. It began
when fellow clergymen attacked him in the press in 1936. Specifically,
the Interdenominational Ministers' Union of Washington proposed
that formal action be taken by that group to "stop Michaux" from
causing damage to the organized Negro church. The statement was
terse, without elaboration on what the nature of that action should
be or exactly how Michaux was damaging the Church. That most
black churchmen regarded him as a cultist partially explains their
attitude toward the Elder, for they believed attacks on the organized
church were intrinsic to cults. Like cultists and sectarians, Michaux
proclaimed his to be a true assembly of God. Any not teaching the
gospel as he did or instituting the same practices, for example, the

organized church that was racially segregated, unemotional, and spiritually cold, programmatically insensitive to religious, social, and political needs and interests of masses, not preaching Bible-centered sermons, not holding up a standard of holiness and sanctification, Michaux called sect, or not true church. Furthermore, because "traditional" denominations were losing members and money to cults and small assemblies during the 1930s but could not or would not meet the challenge of competition by providing more timely and appealing doctrine, services, and programs, it is no wonder that their preachers wanted to stop what they thought was Michaux's offensive.[62] Public attack by his peers raised questions about their credibility and professional standing.

A year later, when Michaux was accused of misappropriating monies from a fund-raising drive, the ministers' protest could be justified by detractors.[63] Whether as a consequence of these circumstances or not the evangelist's popularity slumped, and radio stations canceled options they held on his program and his forum shrank. In September 1938, as Nazi German aggression spread and war clouds formed over Europe, Michaux beamed his second and final broadcast over the BBC.[64] He did not have time, if he had know-how, to regroup, to recapture his radio audience before its attention was preoccupied with the perils and prosperity of World War II. His now predictable radio format no longer was novel entertainment. Moreover, his simple apocalyptic messages, even with "New Thought" flavor, could not sustain the broadcasts in the more sophisticated World War II era of technological advancement, an era when science became a faith alongside religion. Michaux managed to keep his broadcasts on stations where he had churches organized along the East Coast, but after another decade or so, his radio audience consisted almost entirely of members only.

In the disappointment of his decline from radio fame, Michaux surrounded himself with remnants of the glorious past. Features of the new sanctuary in Washington best illustrate this. It had seating capacity of 600 and could accommodate overflow crowds. In recognition of his successful radio ministry, the Elder placed a neon sign atop the church building. It blazoned "Radio Church of God" and carried call letters of the then-defunct station WJSV, where he had begun his radio evangelism.[65]

Anxious to spread the gospel to all the world, Michaux still looked to the media for assistance. Though the radio audience was small, he continued to broadcast weekly, without cessation, and when he died in 1968, his was said to be the longest uninterrupted radio broadcast in U.S. history. He cooperated with commercial firms to cut recordings of broadcasts, and he made these available to the public in the 1940s and 1960s. Realizing the potential of television for his mission, he acquired a program slot on station WTTG and held it for about two years, from 1949 to 1951. He never received popular recognition as a television evangelist, and because of low ratings the program's run was brief.[66]

Among his other efforts at spreading the gospel throughout the world were: Michaux's request that members who were servicemen distribute *Happy News*, the church's twelve-page, monthly tabloid, wherever their tours of duty took them; and his flying to the Bering Strait to drop a Bible, bound inside a metal container, into Russian territory. He envisioned Russia to be a world power but also to be a nation of heathens that could be converted to Christianity if Russians had exposure to the "Word of God" as expressed in the Bible. Ironically, Michaux received a telephone call from an American, some months later, who said he had retrieved the container with the Bible that never had washed onto Russian soil.[67]

Seeking and employing whatever forums and mediums available, Michaux carried out his prophetic mission to the limits of his understanding, ability, and physical strength. In so doing, he not only addressed himself to religious matters but to social and political issues as well.

3

Of Politics and Other Secular Interests

Michaux initially concentrated on meeting religious obligations of his prophetic mission, such as shepherding his flock and spreading the gospel. He later came to understand that in order to successfully fulfill these aspects of the mission, he had to give more than passive recognition to politics and social problems and issues. Consequently, he became more actively involved in social and political causes as it suited his interests to do so. His primary leverage toward this end was the posture of radio evangelist.

The Elder used his radio forum to criticize and/or to praise political leaders, especially presidents, and their practices and policies. He carried, for example, his case against President Herbert Hoover to the millions of his radio listeners. He condemned Hoover for applying pump-priming measures in an effort to revive the economy. Michaux declared that those ineffective measures were to blame, not only for the nation's inability to recover from the Great Depression, but also for its worsening. He advised the president to stop pump-priming big business and to funnel funds directly from the federal government into local communities. As the depression worsened, Michaux became annoyed at Hoover's inability to turn the crisis around, and he accused Hoover of taking his suggestion lightly, of receiving it with mere presidential courtesy.[1]

Advising presidents was serious business to Michaux. He explained that a close relationship between church and state (especially between the Christian church and a democracy) is ideally practical since both should be concerned with advancing the general welfare of the people. Michaux believed, therefore, that presidents should be receptive to utterances from God through prophets. As a result, they would receive proper guidance in recommending and executing democratic policies and practices.[2] Michaux thought his role was one of prophesying, of proclaiming and interpreting God's will to presidents and other national leaders.

His perception of the relationship between himself, as prophet, and political leaders followed in the manner of biblical tradition. From the moment prophecy first appeared in Israel, it was "intimately associated with politics." Prophets were spokespersons for God in times of political crisis, such as war, pestilence, and persecutions.[3] America's earliest black preachers also adhered to this Hebraic tradition. They first emerged in this role during slavery when the slave preacher, and his "free" colleagues like Samuel Ringgold Ward, hoped to raise the social order to a democratic and humanitarian level by preaching against evils of bondage. In later years, Bishop Henry M. Turner and more recently the Adam Clayton Powells, Dr. Martin Luther King, Jr., and Minister Malcolm X also used their pulpits to castigate evils in society and the body politic. It was in keeping with that tradition of prophecy that Michaux addressed a specific social-political plight—the Great Depression.

Conditions were abysmal, even in the nation's capital. Local businesses filed bankruptcy; banks went into receivership. Civil servants were furloughed without pay, and salaries of those still actively employed in government were cut fifteen percent. Thousands were unemployed. Hundreds of families were evicted from their homes. Even the usually dependable Community Chest curtailed aid because its funds were depleted. Congress tried to provide temporary relief to local residents by appropriating emergency doles for the unemployed and for specified resident-families. There were self-help schemes underway, such as family gardening in vacant

lots, a project sponsored by the Council of Social Agencies. Most
of these projects were of limited success because sponsors and participants had difficulty cooperating with each other. People across
the city suffered, but the city's black residents experienced more
widespread destitution because officials parceled out aid on a racially
discriminatory basis, even to mothers of infants and small children.
Furthermore, black migrants, just arriving to the Capital, often
could not meet residency requirements for government assistance
of any kind and were in desperate straits. Despair engulfed the
black community as black Washingtonians tried unsuccessfully
to coordinate available Negro welfare services.[4]

Michaux realized that just criticizing presidential policy and
practice and articulating despair did not absolve him of responsibility
to minister directly to the needy. Though other churches and
denominations made contributions to that cause, Michaux and Father
Divine emerged as the major black organizers of social agencies that
functioned to help meet material needs of the depression's poor. Michaux organized a social welfare program in his Washington church early in 1933. It was one of the most effective private welfare assistance
programs in the Capital. That probably was because the Elder was
one of the few black men in the country with enough clout to successfully fund and operate such a venture. He called the plan the Good
Neighbor League, ironically taking the name from President Hoover's
earlier speech at Fort Monroe in Hampton, Virginia. During the
1932 speech, Hoover asked, "Am I my brother's keeper?" and made
a friendly reference to good neighborliness. Michaux thought the
words "good neighbor" made a "catchy phrase which would attract
followers and make clear his aim" to feed, house, and clothe the
depression indigent, his members' neighbors, in the Washington
area.[5]

The Good Neighbor League launched its activity with a drive to
help the Bonus Army. These 20,000 unemployed World War I veterans
had converged on Washington en masse to urge Congress to make
their bonus certificates negotiable immediately rather than a number
of years later. Lodged in tents on Anacostia Flats and in government
buildings, the "army" was in desperate need. The League raised
over $200 to purchase meat for the hungry veterans, and it gave
them 10,000 pounds of potatoes.[6] These donations made the Church

of God one of the largest black contributors to the Bonus Expeditionary Force.[7] The League also published a weekly paper with a circulation of 75,000 to help the veterans present their cause to the public.[8]

One day Hoover sent troops to run the "army" out of Washington. While carrying out orders, they burned down Michaux's gospel tent. "That day," the Elder exclaimed, "I knew God had rejected Mr. Hoover."[9] So Michaux followed suit. He explained why. When Hoover failed to be counseled by him as God's prophet, he was doomed to corrupt and abusive use of authority. Consequently, he was rejected by God and was to be condemned by God's prophet. To shed further light on his explanation, Michaux cited the biblical story of King Saul.

> God gave to Israel King Saul because they requested a king. He sent Samuel, the prophet, to anoint Saul, king. As long as Saul obeyed God, Samuel, the prophet, commended him to the people. But the day that God commanded Saul to . . . destroy the Amalekites and all their cattle, for they were enemies of Israel, and Saul disobeyed God by sparing King Agag and the best of his flock, God sent Samuel to condemn Saul before the people and to tell him that God had rejected him because he followed not in the footsteps of the commandments of God.[10]

Adhering to that tradition, Michaux immediately began to condemn Hoover as a leader who would not heed God's will on how to end the depression crisis. He advised his millions of radio listeners to vote against the incumbent president and to vote for Franklin Delano Roosevelt. He particularly advised black folk to break customary Republican ties and vote the Democratic ticket. That is why political journalists credited Michaux with using the power of the pulpit to lead "the first swing of Negro voters to the Democratic Party."[11]

Meanwhile operating on other welfare fronts, the Good Neighbor League provided homes for numerous evicted families from around the city in several three-story buildings at Seventh and T streets, NW. A local white attorney, Rudolph Berry, gave the League use of these buildings for one year provided the church group agreed to make them habitable. The church spent thousands of dollars plastering walls, replacing fixtures, windows, window lights, and doors, and papering walls.[12] Seventy or eighty evicted people were moved into those buildings and were said to be "crowded but comfortable, without a landlord to see on Saturday night" as long as they had no income.[13]

Additionally, the League served free and inexpensive but nourishing meals to the hungry in an old MacFadden Café, nearby on Seventh Street. This café, one in a chain of restaurants which sold cheap health foods, had been established by Bernarr MacFadden, the philanthropist and publisher of *Physical Culture* magazine. When the restaurants suffered severe financial losses because of mismanagement and pilfering, MacFadden was prompted to donate the Seventh Street restaurant to Michaux's League.[14] The church renamed it the Happy News Café. Many families ate there, and some individuals received meals in exchange for performing chores around the premises. Michaux asked his radio "audience to send to his café any persons approaching them begging," so he could employ and feed them. "It is better," he instructed, "to help a man help himself than to help him outright." All who came for work were given meal tickets and sent out onto the streets to sell twelve copies of *Happy News*. If they sold the papers, they not only received free meals but also were given free lodging.[15] In a single year, the Happy News Café supplied over 250,000 meals to people around Washington, including 13,140 served to its eighteen regular employees.[16] The café's paying customers increased after the depression, and MacFadden eventually gave Michaux's church the equipment and permanent use of the building.[17]

The Good Neighbor League also operated a free employment service to the dismay of numerous hardpressed, private agencies. Responding to angry statements against the free service, Michaux explained that "He was unable to see why jobless people should be required to pay from $2 to $4 for a job or how they could pay it." Ignoring critics he secured employment for many.[18] Furthermore, he said, in Social Gospel-like fashion, that he boldly entered his church into "the sacred domain of private enterprise in order to help people."[19]

Michaux solicited contributions to finance these philanthropic activities during his broadcasts and on pages of the *Happy News*. Sometimes his listeners responded generously. Once, for example, when he requested $50,000, an unidentified "leading citizen" promptly pledged $35,000 of it.[20] The Elder reportedly received money from people in many parts of the country who were anxious to further his charitable works. However, he noted that he received greatest financial support from employed members of the Church of God, who not only tithed but also gave sacrificial offerings to aid the work.

The League's philanthropy and resultant publicity boosted Michaux's popularity and may have indirectly profited him in other ways. How the outreach affected his church membership rolls is not known. Reportedly, though, "many of the people whom the League aided never set foot inside the Church of God." The church grew during the depression, nevertheless, and some of its new converts may have been beneficiaries of the League's benevolence. There were those who thought Michaux became familiar with congressional legislation and government agencies through his church's social outreach. He would later tap these resources to advance other social and business interests.[21] Whatever benefits Michaux and his church reaped, on balance, they had made significant contributions toward dispelling despair and offering hope for thousands of Washingtonians during the Great Depression.

When newsmen interviewed him about the church's charitable work, the Elder told them that he previously had experimented in that area in Newport News, before ever going to Washington. As early as 1924, the depression gripped his congregation in Tidewater, and he was compelled to devise a plan to keep church doors open and unemployed members fed and housed. Looking back Michaux boasted about the Newport News experiment.

> We came together and began to live on the common plan . . . just as the apostles of old. And we never hungered. . . . All [who lived there, either in the Building on Nineteenth Street and Jefferson Avenue or in another church-owned home on Twenty-second Street] worked and brought their money together every week; we put a big table in the living room and counted it out. Some made $25, $30 . . . Some made $10. Some had no outside employment and so earned no money; we paid all the bills.[22]

Whether or not they could have selected another arrangement, these nearly forty members volunteered to live under this communal plan in order to survive the depression and to help others. Other small religious assemblies and recently organized churches employed similarly effective welfare measures. From the atmosphere of zeal which yet abounded within these groups flowed the Christian spirit of caring and sharing unselfishly so as to prove the presence of God among them. That's why many storefront, holiness, and other "nonnormative" religious groups thrived during the depression while those black churches, long on tradition and short on zeal to practice Christian ideals, nearly went bankrupt. The latter could not, on a whole, effect a meaningful spiritual and material outreach.

Michaux and Elder Howard Poole, the church's treasurer, paid bills for all communal dwellers, and for the church, out of the general pool. They parceled out equal shares of monies left over, usually about four dollars per adult. This share sometimes seemed paltry after a person had contributed thirty dollars or twenty-five dollars and got no more "pocket money" than those who made no monetary contribution. Helpful as it was, to many the arrangement bred resentment.[23] Some cash contributors thought they were being unfairly assessed to help care for families other than their own. One brother, thinking his contributions tremendous, declared that if he ever got off the "plan," he would leave the church home immediately, save his money, and buy himself a house. He had learned that if he could sacrifice that much for the church body, he could do the same to advance himself personally.[24]

In other ways also people were disgruntled, if not with the "plan," per se, at least with its effect on those who participated. Some fellow tenants tended to snoop, watching to see if another member took more than her/his fair share or whatever she/he could eat or drink. They accused each other of hoarding food so they could feed family and friends outside the church. Likewise there were allegations that several members feigned illness to get the church to send them to the doctor and that one of Michaux's sisters was getting more medical attention than other ailing ones.[25]

Fortunately, most members were not fully involved in the Common Plan, so the petty bickering that infected participants was contained. There would not have been enough housing to accommodate all at any rate, and many members chose to remain where they already were buying or renting or to go to live with their biological families. Everyone who was unemployed was eligible to receive free meals from the church's café. In exchange, they cleaned, cooked, washed and ironed for those who worked outside for wages. As the depression worsened, this privilege was extended to unemployed and/or handicapped nonmembers. They "didn't have to say anything but just come on in there and eat . . . not just soup and beans . . . but we gave them plenty of good food. . . . They ate like we did," Michaux recalled. Although these meals were not sumptuous feasts, they were well-balanced, with adequate variety.[26]

Boasting of the Common Plan's effectiveness Michaux said, "Not one member from the Church of God ever went into the bread line."[27] Because he wished this were true his memory had failed him. One member, who was not living on the "plan," was seen standing in a public assistance line to obtain foodstuffs. This was reported to Michaux, and he was livid with anger and chagrin. For that unseemly behavior, causing the church to look like it could not take care of its own, the Elder called the brother before the body and chastised him.[28] In those pre-Social Security and general welfare assistance days, he urged members to depend on the church in times of crisis, not on anyone or any agency outside. The black church had been traditionally the black community's social service and welfare agency, but Michaux was less concerned with tradition than he was with upholding his own church's reputation.

Having extended benevolence to many, the Elder hoped the Christian church in the United States would broaden its base of social welfare outreach to help calm unrest and still fears. Since democracy already had failed the American people in their most desperate moment, he was concerned that Americans might seek communism as an alternative government form. He believed a responsive Christian church could help stem the tide of communism in this country. The Communist party tried to capitalize on desperation resulting from the Great Depression to add to its membership. Party leaders bombarded black neighborhoods, especially, with rallies and ideological rhetoric. They believed black Americans were vulnerable because they suffered abuses of racism as well as momentary ravages of depression, so Communists promised to provide remedy for both. Michaux was so troubled over the Communist presence and the "hope" it held out to black Americans, in particular, that he had a prophecy-dream in the summer of 1933.[29]

In that dream, there were three eagles. The first one was white, representing the National Revival Administration; its program was war on the devil. The second eagle was blue, a symbol of the National Recovery Administration, which was waging war on the depression by establishing hundreds of codes to regulate competition and production in industry and labor. These two eagles were to join forces to fight the third eagle. It was a red one, and Michaux called it the National Revolution Administration, which was waging war on society. He interpreted the dream to mean that he and Roosevelt were to help each other rid the country of political and socioeconomic discontent. It was as a result of this dream that Michaux had prophesied in one sermon, "If we reject the New Deal offered us by God . . . there is nothing left for us but chaos." Believing the New Deal originated with God, the Elder thought it would operate under principles of Christianity. He was optimistic that seeds for a religious revival were part of the program's core and hoped such revival would bring widespread political and social reform. If the American people rejected that program, Michaux believed chaos would result from confusion which the "revolution-oriented Soviets" would foment in the United States. In this anti-Soviet conjecture, he probably was reacting against those Americans who advocated diplomatic recognition of Russia, hoping to increase American trade and to boost the depressed economy. Not recognizing that Japanese expansionism was the major threat to world freedom then, Michaux's primary concern was that the American democracy was in imminent danger of falling prey to Soviet heathenism.[30]

While the Elder interpreted his dream and offered prophecy, Hugh Johnson was drafting NRA codes. Johnson was confident that the new agency would be a practical and beneficial aid to economic planning, but he had misgivings, too. This may indicate why he reacted enthusiastically to Michaux's dream-prophecy.[31] Delighted to have support for NRA from the famous preacher, Johnson arranged a White House appointment to introduce Michaux to Roosevelt.[32] A few months later NRA was invalidated by the Supreme Court

in the Schecter-"sick chicken" case of 1935. But Michaux already
had begun plans to capitalize on the entree to the administration
which the introduction had given him.

He considered that recognition from the presidential appointee to
be a sign that he, a churchman, should take more active interest in
national politics. His initial step in that direction was to write a letter
commending the president on his Brotherhood Day Address from
Hyde Park in 1936. About that speech, which incorporated the
good neighbor concept, Michaux enthused,

> Hello Neighbor, this greeting is sent to you in the spirit of your
> address. . . . In a drive instituted today by the Radio Church of God
> of America to do its part in reviving the good neighbor spirit
> throughout the nation a resolution has been adopted as follows:
> With the usual greeting on meeting which is good morning, the word
> neighbor will be added.[33]

Shortly after sending that telegram, Michaux joined the Good Neighbor League, an organization formed in 1936 to reelect President
Roosevelt.

The Good Neighbor League was the brain child of Stanley High,
a lecturer in religious and current events for the National Broadcasting
Corporation. He was a forty year old native of Chicago. High previously had worked in fields of religion, reform journalism, and
politics. He had earned a divinity degree, and despite his having
never been ordained was pastor of a church in Stamford, Connecticut,
for four years. Like Michaux he had no permanent political loyalties.
Having stumped the country for Hoover in 1928 and 1932, High
was considered to be a Republican. Later, however, he saw much
good in the Democrat's New Deal, and in 1934 High told a group of
students, "The fundamental objective of what we call the New Deal
is religious." He decided to campaign for Roosevelt when he, too,
was inspired by the president's Brotherhood Day Speech. High got
a leave from NBC to work for the incumbent's reelection by organizing
the nonpartisan Good Neighbor League.[34]

Officially launched on April 24, 1936, the League was a coalition
of racial minorities, churchmen, feminists, liberal Republicans, and

loyal Democrats. High went to Washington to solicit the "Happy Am I" preacher's support, and according to Michaux, to get his consent to use the name Good Neighbor League. Michaux cooperated with High, who expressed religious and social sentiments similar to his own, in every way.[35]

The League sponsored rallies in twenty-six major cities throughout the country just to attract black votes. That was in addition to its other campaigning and boosting. This effort was important because most black folk continued to vote Republican through the 1932 presidential election.[36] Michaux, with his Cross Choir, was a major feature at the Madison Square Garden rally. The stage was filled with black bishops, including R. R. Wright, Jr. of the African Methodist Episcopal Church, the influential Baptist preacher Dr. Adam Clayton Powell, Sr., Elder Michaux, along with the Elks Band, Cab Calloway and his orchestra, and W. C. Handy joined them on the platform. There were many grand and inspiring speeches and much exciting entertainment. The "biggest cheer of the evening," though "came at the moment when Michaux dramatically unveiled a vast painting of the 'Three Emancipators'—Abraham Lincoln, Jesus Christ and Franklin Roosevelt."[37] Michaux was overjoyed at the reception and pleased with the recognition that he had gotten as a leading black churchman.

The Elder's role in the Madison Square Garden rally was covered in Washington and New York papers, and he had photographs of himself and the Cross Choir, during their performance, published in *Happy News*. Though campaigning for Roosevelt might have excited Michaux, it did not prove good for him in the long run. Many of his listeners were white and not theologically or ideologically prepared for a politically active evangelist, especially a black one. Recommending that people cast votes for a specific candidate, as Michaux previously had done during broadcasts, was more acceptable.[38] Detractors obviously criticized him for participating in the rally. Two years later, when he was forced to rationalize about his part in that event, he contended that the Garden activity was a religious rather than a political meeting.[39] One wonders how much this single event influenced the decline in his radio audience as publicity circulated.

When the depression was easing off and President Roosevelt's second term was underway, Michaux turned his attention to a problem area outside the United States—Haiti. Exactly why, no one is certain. He heard about that nation's plight from his friend Major Richard R. Wright, who had taken a holiday in Haiti in 1933, following his wife's death. At that time Wright was a Philadelphia banker. He had been president of the Agricultural and Mechanical College of Georgia and was commissioned Paymaster with rank of major during the Spanish American War. He left his Haitian holiday feeling troubled over the extreme poverty among those islanders and pledged to help boost Haiti's economy. Wright initiated an individual effort in that direction by forming the Major Wright Haitian Trading Company to import and distribute Haitian coffee throughout the United States. His firm was the largest importer of that product.[40]

The major wanted to improve the depressed economy of that island nation and discordant U.S.-Haitian relations as well. What role he played, if any, in getting United States troops removed from Haiti is not known. But from 1915 to 1934, U.S. Marines occupied Haitian territory allegedly to insure economic and political stability. After a White House conference between officials from both countries, terms were agreed upon for U.S. troop removal, but agents of U.S. creditors remained in Haiti and prevented autonomy there.[41] Coffee and banana exports to the United States increased in 1935, and the Haitian economy showed signs of improving.[42] By 1936 a considerable amount of the debt to American bondholders was reduced. But yet another crisis occurred when in 1937, the market for Haitian exports fell after Brazil dropped its artificial price ceiling on surplus coffee. Haiti was nearly completely devastated.[43]

Wright, who continued to watch the situation from the United States, discussed Haiti with his friends. Michaux seized that opportunity to form a "good-will" tour group. The delegation of five black men made plans to sail to Haiti ostensibly to determine how its economy could be upgraded.[44] When Michaux informed members of the Roosevelt administration of the group's intended mission, there was considerable interest in diplomatic circles. Under Secretary of State, Sumner Welles, told Michaux "that anything he and his associates could do to increase trade between Haiti and the United States would be something . . . [his] Department would favor enthusiastically and that . . . a 'good-will' trip of [that] kind might be productive."[45] Indicating curiosity, at least, Roosevelt met with the delegation before it sailed. This was a meeting that Michaux had requested. The State Department took steps to secure Haitian approval of the trip, hospitality, and cooperation. It arranged for tours and dinners also. George Gordon, a member of the U.S. Legation in Haiti, "arranged with the President [of Haiti] and with the chief of Protocol for a program of sight-seeing and calls" upon President Vincent, the mayor of Port-au-Prince, and officials of the Chamber of Commerce, and the president invited the group to dine in his home.[46] In addition to Wright, who was president of the Negro Bankers' Association, there were Michaux, and Charles Spaulding, president of the North Carolina Mutual Life Insurance Company, in the group. They represented Negro money, Negro religious appeal, and congregational collateral.

Actually the delegation's agreed upon purpose was to spread "good-will." This agreement was variously defined by them. One unidentified member wanted to create a Haitian market for his soap product.[47] C. C. Spaulding thought the group made the trip to study economic conditions.[48] Wright, realizing that Haiti needed to balance its trade since the United States alone drained off 11 million dollars annually and in return purchased only 1 million dollars worth of Haitian products, wanted to see that country's exports increased. Michaux, who realized that Bishop Lawson's Refuge Church of Christ, for example, had branches in the Virgin Islands and Panama, undoubtedly went to size-up Haiti's possibilities for his church's expansion there.[49]

In any event, the mission was without visible diplomatic value to the State Department. Searching for reasons for what he considered failure, George Gordon found fault with the group's composition. Because one of the men was an insurance official, two were lawyers, and one was a minister, in retrospect Gordon thought the increasing of Haitian-U.S. trade would not be among their top priorities.[50] Haiti's president had not expected this delegation to produce tangible results. He merely issued a postmortem when he said, "Although [I] had been trying all week to elicit some definite suggestion or proposition from [them], [I] completely failed."[51]

These reactions are almost comical in their irony, for the "good-will" group seems to have accomplished, at least to some degree, what it expected. Spaulding reported on economic conditions there to his Durham insurance staff in a series of lectures. Wright increased coffee imports. Michaux did not find Haiti conducive to his church's expansion. His alternative, after that fact-finding trip, was to present himself as altruistic by opening a Haitian café which specialized in Haitian coffee.[52] The café existed only a few months, and Michaux's attention turned to other projects.

The Elder had boundless energy, much hope, and many dreams during the 1930s. The most visionary of his undertakings was the National Memorial to the Progress of the Colored Race of America project. He would locate this memorial alongside what is now the Colonial Parkway (a highway connecting historic Williamsburg and Jamestown) on approximately 500 acres of waterfront and about 1300 acres on the back side (farm land) in James County, Virginia. Michaux purchased the land from an elderly white farmer in 1934. He was proud to have acquired that site "in close proximity to the spot where . . . the first slaves landed" in North America and trusted that the memorial would "develop in the Negro a pride in his race, and . . . educate him in economic independence."[53] He thought these ends could be attained best in "a place where the achievements of . . . Negroes are preserved and held before . . . them."[54]

The memorial was to consist of farm land and beach front, in developed parcels. Architectural designs included a hall of fame (to house portraits, busts, and written materials on black historic figures and contemporary leaders from around the world), a monument to Booker T. Washington, a nondenominational church, a radio station, the Bethune Hostess House, and a statuary group depicting racial progress on the front side of the farm land. Adjoining land on the back side would include a cooperative farm and houses, and an agricultural training center. The beach front would be developed with amusement park and bathing facilities.[55]

Michaux invited prominent black Americans, whom he thought would be sympathetic to the project idea and amenable to using their influence to help advance it, to serve on the memorial advisory board. Emmet Scott (a former Booker T. Washington associate and then Dean at Howard University), Judge James A. Cobb (District of Columbia), A. S. Pinkett (District of Columbia NAACP), Major Wright, William J. Tompkins (Recorder of the Deeds), Mary M. Bethune (a director, National Youth Administration), and Julia West Hamilton (Director, Phyllis Wheatly YWCA) numbered among the board's illustrious members. Each one previously had been cordially supportive of the Elder. They attended his special programs and services and/or invited him to participate in their special functions. Feeling a comfortable relationship to each, Michaux called a board meeting late in 1936 and shortly thereafter began serious planning for developing the memorial site.

His first move was to solicit support of the National Park Service, which operated the Yorktown Historic Park and had interest in the Colonial Williamsburg Restoration. He talked with A. E. Demaray, a Park Service official, about the project. Since Demaray neither endorsed nor opposed the idea, Michaux acted as though the official favored it and suggested to leaders in Tidewater that the Park Service was cooperating. Someone rumored, even, that the Park Service director, Cammerer, had donated monies to the project. Assuming that he had support of a cross-section of black leadership and of a national agency concerned with land development Michaux proceeded to peddle his idea.[56]

He launched what was to have been a nation-wide fund-raising drive in Newport News and Hampton on July 2, 1937, three months after his return from Haiti. To introduce the project to Peninsula residents the Elder placed architectural sketches of the memorial concept on display at the Hampton Normal and Industrial Institute. He explained the concept to groups that gathered at Hampton Institute, and received substantial press coverage in local newspapers. Black and white businessmen, educators, lawyers, ministers, members, and other residents in the area made pledges to the cause.[57] By mid-July some $2,000 in cash had been raised.[58]

Meanwhile the memorial project came under attack from a Park Service official who wanted to confiscate the memorial land and/or relocate the Michaux group. That official was superintendent of the Colonial National Historical Park in Yorktown, Floyd Flickinger He said Michaux was trying to link his Negro memorial to Colonial Park projects and to the Williamsburg Restoration. Flickinger suggested that the Park Service watch for possible foreclosure on the property and that it take action to move the Negro group from that land. He alleged that the memorial "[poses] a serious threat to our development in and around Jamestown." He proposed that a large tract of land "locally known as Fort Eustis, on Mulberry Island . . . be either given or sold to the Negro Memorial [group because that] location is off the beaten track for the majority of our Park visitors."[59] Cammerer, in response to Flickinger, showed less obvious consternation. "As a Federal officer," he wrote, "I . . . cannot take any active sides in this matter nor should you." He continued, pointing out that he could not see how the memorial could be considered a detriment to the Colonial Historic Park or to the Jamestown unit "simply because it is sponsored by the Colored Race. The proponents of this project have every right to plan for a memorial on their property." Cammerer added that Park Service officials should only hope memorial plans would be in harmony with Park Service projects in the area. But hearing that Michaux had discussed his plans with Vernon Geddy in Williamsburg and had so impressed him that Geddy was taking the matter to Rockefeller, the annoyed Flickinger would not leave the matter alone. He continued to urge displacement of the Negro group from that prime land and received unexpected help in squelching the project.[60]

Michaux had not called a board meeting since late 1936, and board members, on whose names he capitalized during promotional activities and fund-raising, began to complain. Some complained publicly, saying the National Memorial plan was "only . . . a real estate promoter's project." They accused Michaux of not giving them accountings of fund-raising progress and showed suspicion of his financial activities.[61] Their suspicion on that front was not surprising since it was generally known that certain black religious leaders had acquired great wealth by the mid-1930s from contributions of people sympathetic to their causes. Conspicuous consumption was equated with opulence, as when Bishop Emmanuel C. Grace (founder, House of Prayer for All People), for instance, purchased a "sumptuous country estate and fruit farm" in Cuba in 1936. *Ebony* magazine carried photos of the palatial estate and a story, stating that the bishop paid more money for the property than realtors had been requesting.[62] As a black, self-proclaimed prophet-showman and founder of his own religious organization,

Michaux often was identified with exotic malefactors, and his unaccountability in financial matters made him all the more suspect. The board's statements to the press discredited the Elder and the memorial project. As a result, Michaux terminated the fund-raising effort.[63]

Although his project had stalled, Michaux held onto the memorial land. But, according to his recollection years later, National Park Service officials seized upon an idea that he earlier had proposed to harrass him and to try to wrest away the land. Michaux said he had suggested to Demaray late in 1936, about the time of the National Memorial board meeting, that the federal government construct a road to link the National Memorial land to Jamestown and to Williamsburg. No matter what the source of this idea, Demaray, who in 1930 was acting director of the Park Service, decided that a parkway should be constructed to connect the two historic areas. That decision caused Michaux years of headache after Congress passed a bill for the parkway.[64] When that bill passed, Michaux was thrown into a six-year (1939-45) fight with the Park Service whose agents specified that beach front of the memorial land be confiscated to make way for the thoroughfare. The Elder was incensed by what he perceived to be a change in Park Service policy toward his project and he fought back.

To protect the real estate Michaux engaged Attorney Clarence J. Owens, who, if not then, previously had ears of folk who were prominent in national political circles. Owens had held several presidential commissions. He was a member of the commission that Charles Dawes headed to help settle debts of nations and post-World War I reparations. Owens was appointed in 1913 by Woodrow Wilson as director general of the Federal Farm Loan System. He was past commander-in-chief of the Sons of Confederate Veterans and was lieutenant colonel in the Army. Most significantly to Michaux's case, however, was Owens' previous appointment by the Department of the Interior to a commission regarding the Yorktown Historic Park. Moreover, Owens was negotiating with the Department of the Interior for several other large property owners in the Williamsburg-Jamestown area, as for example, the Williamsburg Coal Company and Dr. G. L. Smith, who owned waterfront property known as Sprately Farm and Archer's Hope.[65]

Owens and Michaux made an interesting duo. Both were tenacious, unyielding sorts, determined to win battles. From December 1938 to December 1939, Owens peppered Ickes and Park Service officials with information and sermons showing how pro-New Deal Michaux was. In one letter, Owens cautioned Ickes that "the Party lost one of the foremost leaders of the Negro Race recently by failure to heed the advice of Elder Michaux."[66] If they did not give Michaux a fair hearing and equitable settlement, more support for the administration would be lost, he implied. Eventually Owens became caustic in his approach after the Park Service offered him, as "a friend of the Department of the Interior," a buffalo skin, as if to obligate him to the department or prejudice him in the cases.[67] Failing to make satisfactory headway Owens sent Ickes a pamphlet warning him that Communist agents were in the government, and he sent Assistant Secretary of the Department of the Interior Chapman a letter, declaring:

> You and Demaray have gone out of your way to try to destroy a great program [the National Memorial project] and have not hesitated to endeavor to injure me. . . . The facts of the Dies Committee are only incidental to the facts in my possession.
>
> When I endeavored to have you consider the public service of Elder Michaux and his fidelity to the Administration that gave you your high place, you stopped me, and now I will be willing to put the character and the patriotism of the Elder up against your standards at any time.

Implying that Chapman was a Communist, he continued, "There are others, as you know, who are listed with the 563 that have been classified" as Communists by the Dies Committee.[68] For that bit of implied defamation, Ickes terminated correspondence with Owens, forcing him off the case. Michaux engaged Attorney Nathan Boone Williams at the recommendation of Owens.[69]

Negotiations stalled around the fact that Michaux would not agree to sell 38.6 acres of memorial land for less than $8,940 plus 2,000 feet of beach front that would be conditioned by the Park Service to prevent washing and right-of-way to easements on each side of the parkway. So the department filed condemnation proceedings against the memorial land.[70] Michaux refused to yield and contended with these officials until he won a point.

Meanwhile, he busied himself with another real estate venture—the Mayfair Mansions housing project in Washington. After the war ended, almost as suddenly as the difficulty with the Park Service and Department of the Interior had surfaced, it was settled in the Elder's favor in 1945. He sold 39.55 acres of the memorial land so the parkway could progress and received a cash settlement of $10,000, plus easements from the parkway onto memorial land, and continued use of the beach front that was conditioned by the Park Service. But only time would determine who really was winner of that contest, for an ominous clause was in the settlement: The beach front remained under control of the memorial group for perpetuity so long as no unsightly structures were placed along it, at which time the Park Service could force the group to relinquish "control."[71] The Park Service would determine what was unsightly and when to wrest the property from Michaux and his organization, so the "victory" was of dubious value in the long run.

Few persons, other than Michaux and his attorneys, followed details of this drama with the National Park Service. Most people, who would have been interested, did not have enough dialogue and scenes from the drama to make sense of what was happening. Members neither knew about nor understood what the litigation entailed or the settlement foretold since Michaux did not inform them of details. He would give vague mention of the litigation and move on to another matter.[72]

Michaux never was able to revive support for the memorial project mainly because he had not aroused a popular front of black interest. Most black folk, who initially were interested, lost concern when it became clear to them that Michaux intended the memorial to be a Church of God project. Though he was clever enough to "save" the land at that time, he was not astute enough to fashion his modus operandi in such a way as to convince black Americans that the memorial could be a community effort and project. The memorial concept never was implemented, but it remained hauntingly alive for Michaux until he died, and supporters who kept certificates of shares, purchased in 1936, have constant reminders of the failure.

Michaux was challenged by the full range of needs of human beings whose spiritual longings partly reflected social alienation. Therefore, he tried to extend his ministry across the spectrum of problems and concerns confronting the socially disinherited ones. Through self-help programs, political persuasion, economic development, and by focusing on black achievements, he aspired to stake a claim for fuller black participation in American society. Because of this all-encompassing goal, his interest extended to presidents as contributors to the authorship of American public policy and action.

4

The Prophet and the Presidents

Following the decline of his powerful radio pulpit Michaux re-adjusted his approach to the wielding of power. Anxious to perpetuate his image as an internationally prominent preacher, despite set-backs and disappointments, he succumbed to self-aggrandizement and currying favor with presidents. This approach to power and recognition is detectable in the Elder's correspondence with Presidents Roosevelt, Truman, and Eisenhower and in his attitude toward and "attacks" upon other black religious leaders. This dedication to self-promotion became obvious during President Roosevelt's re-election campaign of 1940.

Michaux attended the Democratic National Convention that year and secured a place on the program to make a nominating speech. With dignified bearing and characteristically rapt facial expression, he addressed the body in a manner suggesting that he still enjoyed the widespread influence of a national radio pulpit. "As leader of the people," he boasted to the delegates,

... the colored people of America. . . . [I am] authorized by the
delegates of the State of Happy Minds to nominate Mrs. . . . Roosevelt
. . . [,] wife of the greatest President who ever lived, for Vice-President.
. . . The number of delegates . . . consist of those of my race that
are protected from social injustice by the Social Security Act, old age
pension, . . . the NYA, the WPA, and who have a little savings in
safe banks.[1]

This self-appointed representative of "colored people" had equated
social justice with economic security, but he did not raise questions
dealing with the issue of government guaranteed economic security
nor those referring to his previous concern with the issue of self-help.
Receiving no satisfactory response from the convention or from the
"colored people" and black leadership, he followed-up that address
with a telegram to the president. Michaux reported that "After
sitting in the . . . Convention . . . listening to the delegates . . . and
also to your acceptance speech [,] . . . I was moved to call the seven
churches over which I am overseer in special prayer to God for your
health and strength." Indicating that he was in the vanguard with
that deed, the Elder continued, "We trust that other churches will
follow the example."[2] On the face of it, this surfaces as one more
of Michaux's ingratiating overtures to the president, for he calls
attention to how he and his several churches are praying special
prayers for Roosevelt. Yet, there might have been genuine Christian
ministry involved here on the Elder's part. In a 1948 letter to Eisenhower, he said President Roosevelt told him he feared death was
imminent.

Michaux took the opportunity, nevertheless, to inform the president of his continuous support and of his influence which made that
support valuable. He wanted to wield power, sometimes to achieve
an immediate goal. A relationship is detectable, for example, between
Michaux's overtures to President Roosevelt and his confiscation
case against the National Park Service that was pending from 1939
to 1945. Michaux was determined to receive a favorable decision.
Therefore, he courted the president, the Secretary of the Interior,
Ickes, and others in the Roosevelt administration in an effort to
influence the decision. Sensibly, with the war underway, he made
declarations of support and praise for the president rather than

disapprobation. The tactic paid off, and when a settlement favorable
to Michaux was rendered in the fall of 1945, spectators mused that
prior to dying Roosevelt intervened in the Elder's behalf.[3]

Michaux's gentle offensive, which prevailed over Attorney Owens'
more aggressive approach, was sensible for two other reasons. He
was building a federally subsidized housing project, Mayfair Mansions, beginning in 1942 and to bring it to successful completion he
needed to keep channels of communication and cooperation open
to the administration. That same year he also had a legal suit pending
against the government for alledgedly obstructing free enterprise.
Michaux believed the movie he and Jack Goldberg compiled, "We've
Come A Long, Long Way," received unfair competition in theaters
from the government film, "Why We Fight." The latter was a popular
war movie showing a dossier of mistreatment and discrimination
against black soldiers in the South. Because of its popularity, Michaux found it difficult to get his film booked for showing. While
the New York court did not enjoin the government to stop distrib-
uting its film, the Elder got clearance to run his film in various cities
before the government's movie was shown.[4] Michaux's approach to
entanglement with the federal government was pragmatic. He had
learned years before that he could receive favor from the Roosevelt
administration by being supportive rather than hostile to it. When
the black Washington Industrial Savings Bank was reopened in
1933, after the bank holiday under a provision that depositers be
paid only thirty-five percent of their frozen deposits, many Washingtonians considered that a favor extended to Michaux in recompense
for support of party and administration. That reopening was irregular,
for under terms of the Emergency Bank Act, the Treasury Department rarely permitted banks to become re-active before they could
make at least a fifty percent pay-off to customers who had lost
deposits. Since Michaux was a major client with the ISB, black
folk, in particular, credited his influence in high places for that coup.
That such recompense, real or illusory, was whispered about the
community was a boost to Michaux's sense of worth.

The Elder's efforts to curry favor with President Truman tend
toward the dramatic. After he spent much time contending with
them, Democratic officials grudgingly permitted Michaux to join
at the end of the 1948 presidential victory parade. He joyfully entered

the procession with a bandwagon, proclaiming, "God did it and we thank Him." The wagon, a pick-up truck's flat-bed, was decorated with Michaux's perennially used red, white, and blue bunting, with loudspeakers and posters, heralding the fulfillment of the Elder's prophecy that Truman, the underdog, would be elected. Dressed in long black robe and skull cap, Michaux stood beside the Democratic Party's symbolic donkey as he thanked God for the victory. This drama can be understood better by flashing back to the first of the year in order to follow Michaux's unofficial, self-assumed role in Truman's presidential campaign.

In January 1948, Truman granted the Elder, and other representatives from the National Freedom Day Association, an audience. Michaux had requested the appointment ostensibly so the group could present the president a photograph of the Association's founder, the late Major Richard R. Wright, Sr. Besides Michaux, those in attendance were Emmanuel C. Wright (one of the major's sons) and Emmet Jay Scott.[5] Conversation other than an exchange of strict formalities between the delegation and the president as the presentation was made is unknown. There is no evidence that Truman's impending candidacy was discussed. Curiously, though, on the very next day, Michaux announced to the Washington press his decision to support the incumbent for election. His audience with Truman had been as part of a delegation, but the announcement was issued independently, without mention of the National Freedom Day Association.[6] Exploration of why he made this move is mere conjecture, but some members of the church believed he and Truman had conferred about the president's political future, that the president had "solicited" Michaux's support, and that God had directed the Elder to back the incumbent. Others did not know what to think; therefore, they accepted Michaux's decision on face value and were supportive of him because they wanted to be loyal to leadership.[7]

In June, Michaux sent a letter to General Eisenhower, with a message for Truman, and forwarded a copy to the President. He wrote in reaction to draft-Ike-feelers which were then underway in both of the two major parties. Assuming his stance as prophet, the Elder explained why Truman would be elected and why Eisenhower should not run for president in 1948:

Under the direction of the Spirit of God, I write you this letter. It was under the guidance of the holy prophets of old that God made sure and unfailing the steps of men who were ordained by Him to lead His people. . . .

There will be a move on to draft you for the presidency, and God has ordained that you be, but not until Mr. Truman's time expires. Mr. Truman is God's anointed for the position he now holds; [sic] for he was not placed there by any political party but by Divine Providence . . . brought about by the death of Mr. Roosevelt.

President Truman has done a wonderful job up to this time in holding together the platform and principles that were set by God through the late Mr. Roosevelt which selfish Democrats and Republicans have attempted to destroy. . . .

God moved Mr. Roosevelt to choose [Truman] as his successor in case of his death, which God made him to know, for he told me personally of his fears.

Under divine inspiration, I suggest that you should decline the presidency (if you are drafted . . .) and accept the position as running mate of Mr. Truman. . . .

Furthermore, Michaux advised Eisenhower that since Truman was elevated by God, he was locked into that position for seven consecutive years. He was responsible to God and not to a political party. Therefore, Truman must heed advice of God through His prophet, Michaux, as Roosevelt had. Alluding to his own NRA prophecy, Michaux wrote, "I was the late Mr. Roosevelt's prophet. We never failed God. Through us God broke all precedence to carry out His purpose to lift up the common people and show His love to them."

Michaux clearly would not allow himself to separate the Roosevelt and Truman administrations, from 1944 to 1948. He concluded the letter with characteristic references to his important accessibility to presidents. "I am going to personally place a copy of this letter in the President's hand this week," he confided.[8]

Three days later, Michaux telephoned the White House to request that a delegation from the National Freedom Day Association be present on June 30 when the president would sign a Joint Resolution of Congress. The resolution declared February 1 "Emancipation Day" in the United States. Black folk in various parts of the country celebrated it at different times, according to when slaves in an area first heard about emancipation, rather than uniformly on January 1 which was the date that the Emancipation Proclamation was effected in 1863. Via some dubious formula and combination of factions, February 1 was offered in 1948. Because this was a resolution affecting a black day of celebration, when Michaux telephoned, he advised a White House aide that "it would be awfully good publicity to . . . have . . . [a black delegation] photographed when the President sign[s] the Bill . . . since all the Negro papers would carry" the story and photograph.[9] Truman not only honored that suggestion but he also flattered Michaux on that occasion by asking for a copy of the "Three Emancipators" cartoon.[10]

The Elder was increasingly satisfied with Truman's behavior. When he created a committee on civil rights early in 1948, Michaux was convinced of Truman's commitment to the spirit of the New Deal. At the time of establishing that committee the president had said, "I want our Bill of Rights implemented in fact. We have been trying to do this for 150 years. We are making progress but we are not making progress fast enough."[11] Truman proposed that Congress pass legislation to abolish segregation and discrimination in transportation and insisted that a strong civil rights plank be included in the 1948 Democratic platform. Circumstances combined in that moment to make Michaux, simultaneously, loyal to race and president.

To his public it looked like Michaux, the prophet, was taking a great risk by so openly throwing his support to the president. He seemed to be in a predicament. Spring public opinion polls revealed that hardly more than one-third of the voters favored the Truman candidacy. The incumbent was losing the "solid" South's support of the Democratic Party because he had raised the issue of civil rights to a national level. But Michaux, who was not inclined to take public positions that were unpopular unless he thought they strengthened his authority, could hardly have done less than support Truman. Counting himself among its leadership, he did not want to be held in contempt in the black community by not endorsing the candidate that it believed would give a fair deal. Complementing, yet overriding this consideration, was Michaux's belief that God had ordained Truman to be president for seven years. He dared believe, as he hoped, Truman would win.

Undaunted in the face of pollsters' dire predictions for a Dewey victory Michaux campaigned vigorously for Truman. He broadcasted a pro-Truman election rally. Chimes sounded and an announcer bellowed, "Prophet and prophetic words!" Then there was a reading from Amos 3:5–8, telling of how the Lord does nothing without first revealing to prophets that it will be done, and Michaux said that God revealed to him that Truman would be elected in 1948. To emphasize God's anointing of Truman, Michaux interpreted the names Dewey and Truman. He said Dewey signified chaos while Truman denoted salvation. Dewey would vanish under heat. "If Dewey is elected," Michaux warned, "our government will vanish under pressure from Russia" because Communists will infiltrate labor unions, causing strikes and depression which will lead to revolution. Truman is a substitute to the people for Roosevelt. Then Michaux called for laborers, Negroes, and Jewish people to go to the polls to vote for Truman.[12]

In the end, black voters played a significant part in Truman's election. Michaux had suggested that significance in June. Henry Lee Moon, the NAACP's Public Relations Director, speculated early in 1948 that the black vote in certain pivotal states could swing close national elections. He based this projection on figures showing the "steady migration of Negroes to the North and West and their concentration in important industrial communities." This would undoubtedly give "them a new powerful voice in political affairs."[13] Approximately 75 percent of the three million black Americans who voted cast ballots for Truman.[14] It is possible that a 15 percent switch in black votes in California, Illinois, and Ohio would have thrown the election to Dewey.[15]

After Truman won, Michaux celebrated by parading in the streets of Washington. He was ecstatic because his prophecy had been fulfilled. Members from across the field of churches were excited. Some leaped for joy because the prediction had come to pass, and many were refreshed in faith by that validation of Michaux as prophet.[16]

Michaux's visible interest in the presidential campaign of 1948 was not altogether altruistic. His converging financial and political concerns indicate that he wanted to prove himself to be influential in order to receive certain financial considerations. Mortgage payments on his large housing project in Washington were in arrears. He wanted to borrow enough money from the Reconstruction Finance Corporation to make the mortgage current and to expand the project's operations. In 1949 the RFC loan was negotiated despite the history of delinquent payments, and one prominent black Washingtonian inferred that Truman had used his influence to help Michaux obtain that loan.[17]

Because he had met the Eisenhowers in their pre–White House years, Michaux tried to establish a relationship of camaraderie with President Eisenhower. He presumed that he was recognized by that family as a long-time friend, not as a mere acquaintance. That presumption resulted from his having been introduced to Mrs. Mamie Eisenhower during the early 1940s after he sent a Sister Mary Newton from the church to work for her. Empathizing with this woman whose husband was away at war, Michaux began to direct his Washington congregation in prayers for the general, and he sent Eisenhower a letter informing him of this early in 1945.[18] He wrote to the general again toward the end of 1945 to inform him that the Radio Church of God had named him an honorary deacon and sent a Bible to seal the appointment. Eisenhower responded with an autographed picture of himself "in appreciation" of the Elder's assistance in the country's war effort. But the general did not acknowledge the honorary deaconship.[19] Despite its curt formality, this response encouraged Michaux to woo Eisenhower, and he proceeded in that manner by recommending that the general should become president.

Michaux bragged to members that he was the first person to mention the presidency to Eisenhower. But the general credited Virgil Pinkley, a newspaper correspondent in the North African Theater during 1943, with broaching the subject. Pinkley had reminded him at the time that war heroes often were elected to the presidency.[20] Eisenhower made no mention at all of Michaux in his memoirs, and the earliest evidence of correspondence between them is dated 1945, some two years after the date of the Pinkley conversation. Michaux's presumption that Eisenhower shared his perspective on the matter forced the commanding tone of the 1948 letter in which he urged Eisenhower not to run that year.

When Michaux began to follow Eisenhower's presidential campaign with relish and support in 1952, people called him an opportunist.

Some recalled how he had entreated black folk to break with the Republican Party in 1932 and again in 1936, and they noted how supportive the Elder had been of the two Democratic administrations through almost twenty years. For those reasons, they thought he was a Democrat. Michaux, though, earlier clarified for Eisenhower how he stood on the issue of loyalty to one party. He had written to the general saying, "As I told you when I was with you last in your office; [sic] God did not need a Republican or Democrat. . . . He needs . . . a man."[21] Michaux proceeded to show everyone that he was nonpartisan by promoting Eisenhower for president instead of the Democratic candidate, Adlai Stevenson.

After Eisenhower was elected, Michaux sent him letters and telegrams frequently on the basis of a presumed friendship. The president's staff sent the Elder courteous replies of acknowledgement. Invitations to visit the White House did not follow as Michaux hoped they would, however. Reflecting disappointment, he sent Mrs. Eisenhower this advice: Her husband should not run for another term although he had done a "wonderful job in a very short time." Michaux continued on to explain that he thought the president already had fulfilled his mandate from God by "stopping the Korean War" and by trying to desegregate Washington.[22] He obviously was annoyed with the president for not giving him recognition he thought he deserved as a family "friend." The Elder undoubtedly was even more chafed when recalling that several members were outspoken in their opposition to his support of the Eisenhower presidential campaign. He realized the general was unpopular among the black electorate mainly because he had endorsed the Army's Jim Crow policies during World War II. He also knew that his members expected him to receive an invitation to visit the White House to chat and pray with his long-time "friend" whom he helped get elected. Michaux was uneasy about the cold-shoulder. He continued, nevertheless, to send prayer telegrams and sermons to the president, for to have done less would have been direct admission of unease and opportunism.

When Eisenhower suffered a heart attack in 1956, Michaux held a special prayer meeting for him. That struck a sensitive chord, and the president responded by inviting the Elder to visit him. But the president cautiously had a memo recorded to explain that he extended the invitation so he could thank Michaux for the all-night prayer meetings.[23] Michaux, his own, ever ready, public relations man, carried a copy of *Sparks from the Anvil* to Eisenhower with whom he posed for photographs, along with Mrs. Michaux and Ieeda, the Eskimo girl from Alaska (see note 10, chap. 1). That visit received newspaper coverage, giving the Elder the genre of publicity he could tailor to benefit his power play.[24] Subsequently, Michaux changed his mind and decided Eisenhower should run for reelection, and again he enthusiastically campaigned for his incumbent "friend."

At the Annual Baptizing that September, the Elder displayed a six-foot photograph of the Eisenhowers and captioned it "Our Peace-loving President and His Wife." Then he sent a copy of an article, about that ball park service, from the *Washington Post* to the president. The article included, of course, information about the huge gathering at that year's Baptizing.[25] Michaux did other campaigning, too, in 1956, though not officially for the Republican Party. He went to Detroit and Pontiac to visit with a Church of God in Christ traveling evangelist—his friend Elder Oren B. Rhodes, who often conducted revivals in Michaux's churches. While there, he made speeches to get "the rest of [those] colored Democrats . . . [interested in returning] to their first love—the Republican Party." Ignoring earlier complimentary epithets to Presidents Franklin Roosevelt and Truman, he called Eisenhower the "Second Emancipator." The Elder said Eisenhower had "done more for the Negro in the last four years than . . . the presidents who have been in office in the past twenty years." He took that message to Flint, Saginaw, Bay City, Pontiac, and Lansing, Michigan and sent copies of press releases covering his tour back to Washington to the president.[26]

A week before he went to Michigan, Michaux broadcasted a sermon entitled "Who Will Be Elected—Mr. Eisenhower or Mr. Stevenson?" He answered the question with a resounding "No!" for Stevenson. But carefully pointed out that he was no political adviser to Eisenhower, and he even publicly disavowed his having political influence upon the president. In a radio sermon, he insisted, "Since my visit to the White House many people asked me, 'Do you think . . . Eisenhower will be elected?' Because of my constant visits to presidents, they think I'm a politician. I'm not a politician; I'm a prophet . . . When I went to the White House, I didn't talk politics, I talked about Heaven."[27] While he implied his mission as God's spokesman to presidents, Michaux showed himself to be resigned to the fact that he could not flaunt the posture of prophet-adviser on politics to Eisenhower without becoming persona non grata at the White House.

Although he made a $50 donation in 1957 for a mural in the reno-vated Washington church, Eisenhower extended Michaux no oppor-tunity to manuever unguardedly within the bounds of their acquaint-ance.[28] That the president responded to him with distant formality was disconcerting to the Elder. In a final comment on that admin-istration, he vented disgust as he announced disapprobation upon the Eisenhower-Khrushchev conference of August 1961. He declared that conciliatory meeting a "sad day," for the Elder was afraid the president would compromise democratic principles before the leader of a communist nation.[29]

By publicizing whatever recognition he received from the presi-dent, the Elder appeared to be a man of influence in important quarters. He felt the need for the public to associate him with presidents so he could create leverage from that image, however illusory, to command funds and fiscal decisions that would help him develop and protect his properties. That appearance of influence created sufficient clout to prevent his prosecution for back taxes on the housing project and to avert foreclosure because of delinquent mortgage payments on the same. Michaux retained traces of youthful audacity. Faced with huge financial obligations and impending foreclosures, he applied for a loan to build another housing project in 1960.[30]

After Eisenhower left office in 1961, Michaux could no longer claim, with credibility, to have the ear of the president nor to have access to the White House. A new, powerful group of black leaders emerged out of the civil rights movement of the late 1950s and early 1960s, and a new breed of preachers like Dr. King gained unprece-dented access to the youthful President Kennedy. These politically active preachers were heralded as prophets and could gather crowds almost instantaneously to hear them speak or preach. Michaux was visibly displaced, and he reacted unkindly to the displacement by not supporting civil rights and black social promotion groups. There was one exception—the National Freedom Day Association. It was founded by his friend, Major R. R. Wright, Sr., to celebrate annually the passage of the Thirteenth Amendment. That organiza-tion afforded Michaux the opportunity to associate with leading black Americans, such as Channing H. Tobias, Rufus E. Clements, John W. Davis, Bishop David H. Sims, Charles Wesley, Benjamin Mays, Horace Mann Bond, Rayford Logan, and the novitiate— Martin Luther King, Jr.[31] The Elder honed associations of this sort to his own advantage, using pages of *Happy News* to bring them to attention of members, other subscribers, and all else whom he wanted to impress with his contacts. Besides, his personal relationship with the major, like that with Judge Cobb (of Washington), was one of a handful which bore resemblance to friendship. Michaux and Bishop Sims, though, did establish a camaraderie of sorts that lasted through Sims' suspension from the prelacy in the African Methodist Episcopal Church in 1946, and the Elder permitted several other such loose associations to form. His relationship with Major Wright was so close, however, and the major was indulgent enough of him that Michaux could project an image of foremost leadership, to those whom he elected to impress, in the National Freedom Day Association. With its assortment of black intellectuals, educators, religious leaders, financiers, and jurists this was a formidable body, and Michaux's projected image of leadership benefitted his interests. Wherever his projected posture of authority and foremost leadership was ignored, threatened, or not indulged Michaux often became detractor.

He vehemently criticized black nationalists and civil rights groups, for example, because he could not presume to effect influence over philosophies they espoused and activities they promoted. So the Elder based his detraction upon the rationale that their activities contributed to further racial polarization, rather than assume a neutral stance. Yet, his staged spectacular to denounce the popular Nation of Islam was exceptional behavior, even for Michaux. He arranged a debate between himself and Elijah Muhammed in Griffith Stadium, during the Sunday series leading to the Baptizing of 1961, and denounced the "Messenger," calling him leader of a "cult of hate."[32] Michaux had gone to such lengths partly out of anger and frustration with his brother whom he could not whip back in line. This brother, Louis, sometimes fondly called "Professor Michaux" by writers and avid readers of black literature who frequented his Harlem bookstore, had worked closely with the Elder until well into the 1940s. Recently he had formed a close relationship to and admiration for Malcolm X. Louis' touting of Minister Malcolm was taken to be an affront by the Elder, and he set out to expose and discredit the Muslim movement. The well-publicized confrontation turned out to be a plum in terms of attendance. Crowds, such as had not turned out for a Michaux affair since the 1940s, attended to behold the spectacular Muhammed-Michaux debate.[33] It portended to be a debacle for the Elder, for in its wake, he was labeled a racial conservative by many witnesses and receded further into the national background.

Members, who disagreed with the venomous sting of Elijah Muhammed's antiwhite mouthings and cringed before his anti-Christian philosophy, found much to admire in the "Messenger's" forthright attacks on racial discrimination and economic exploitation in this country. They saw Dr. King as a symbol of the struggle against all racism and discrimination and held him in high esteem. They were pleased, therefore, when Michaux lauded King, calling him a "Saint" on the front page of a *Happy News* paper.[34] That was the highest honor the Elder ever bestowed upon anyone outside his church, and within the church saint was an expression reserved for "sin-free" members. That post-1963 March-on-Washington praise did not last long, though, for Michaux soon found opportunity to criticize King. The very next year he sent King an open letter, reproving him for having accused J. Edgar Hoover of dereliction of duty in not bringing civil rights violators in Georgia to justice. Hoover was one of Michaux's acquaintances, who in light of recent revelations about his operations might have stayed his hand when some of the Elder's financial dealings could have been "exposed" to public investigation. At any rate, Michaux offered a defense of his "friend" against King's attack. In that letter, Michaux told King that he had personally investigated his complaints against Hoover and had found them baseless. Michaux explained naively that the FBI served as an investigatory body and left local government to punish and maintain law and order. The letter cited civil rights investigations conducted by the FBI and the positive results, based on the Elder's evaluation. In 1964 alone, Michaux wrote, the FBI investigated 3,340 civil rights violations, and Dr. King had not done his homework before speaking out. "Your statement based on suspicion only," Michaux counseled, "was a grave error . . . and Mr. Hoover, knowing the strenuous efforts . . . put forth by his department to do all in [its] power to bring every violator of Civil Rights to justice was provoked to call you a notorious liar."[35] Michaux said King, as recipient of the Nobel Peace Prize, should apologize to Hoover, and both men should "bury the hatchet that could result in America's downfall."[36]

While there is no evidence that either man responded to Michaux, he would not leave the matter alone. In an interview for Virginia's conservative Chamber of Commerce magazine, *Commonwealth*, he warned with an air of righteous indignation, "Unless the policy of Martin Luther King is curbed, we are in for trouble. I don't approve of King's manner of defying local government. He must conform to local government."[37] That politically conservative statement certainly was inconsistent with Michaux's own behavior some forty years earlier, when he had defied Virginia's racial segregation laws and practices. In his own youthful defiance, the Elder, like King, also argued that state laws are superceded by a Higher Order of Law. This causes one to wonder why Michaux sent that letter to King and why he made it public. To leave it as a "favor" to Hoover is not enough.

He had "taken King to task" and publicized that fact. This indicates that the Elder was bothered by King, for there is no other known instance in which he reacted to black leaders in that manner. It seems reasonable to suspect that his motive was cloaked in yet another statement to the *Commonwealth* reporter. "His methods are getting publicity for him but not for the human race." The key word is publicity. No black preacher before King had received national or international prominence and acceptance to the extent that it forced Michaux to confront his own displacement and obscurity. Others had not had as widespread white as well as black following and support. With King's ascendancy, Michaux saw clearly that his days of prominence and usefulness were ended. King had employed a Christian gospel, demonstrations, and tactics of civil disobedience to force the United States to give more than lip service to tenets of democracy and Christianity. That activity was reminder to Michaux that for years he, too, had urged the nation and its leaders to adhere to Christian and democratic principles. Michaux and members picketed and marched around the White House, cathedrals, churches, subway stations, and along busy streets, usually in Washington and New York City. They had dramatized discontent in this manner through the years. In 1961, for example, they dressed in burlap sacks and caps, hung signs around their necks and picketed, calling for the Church in America to "Repent" and "Unite" Christian efforts in social reform. The group gathered on the lawn of the National Monument where that Thanksgiving Day activity culminated.[38] Michaux saw a nation, which was oblivious to his warnings, heed King's cry and demonstrations. King succeeded where Michaux failed, so the aging Elder, out of egotistical frustration, lashed out at the "upstart." Hence, he sent the startling open letter to the beloved leader whose civil disobedience tactics even Michaux's members admired. The letter did not serve Michaux well either inside or outside his church. Members were chagrined, and many privately questioned the Elder's judgement. Some of the new generation of black Americans across the country who heard about the incident asked, "Who is Michaux?" The matter, where not completely ignored, was shrugged off by the avaricious press and by the populace which always awaits periodic media feedings of sensationalism.

While it is not unusual for anxiety to follow one's decline from prominence, the transition was especially difficult for Michaux because he basked in the star treatment. People recognized the power of his radio pulpit and sought him out for help in promoting causes and projects. The Reverend Jardine, the English cleric who married the former King Edward and Wallis Simpson, for instance, went to seek Michaux's influence in publicizing a movie that attacked sexy pictures.[39] One reporter accurately captured the image that Michaux struggled to perpetuate when he wrote, "He has government officials under delusion, for they think he speaks for all Negro denominations."[40] The Elder was unable to graciously accept the limited influence set by his decline from radio fame. Consequently, he tried continuously to project an image of powerfulness. It was toward that end that he curried favor with presidents and criticized popular black preachers. He was self-aggrandizing, resembling one gripped in internal struggle with his identity. But he always understood that there was a relationship between his influence potential and the size of his membership and followers. The Elder, therefore, designed measures to maintain reins of control over his most valuable asset—his members.

1. **Michaux Early in His Ministry.** This photograph was taken in about 1930.

2. **Michaux Preaching Over the Radio.** This photograph shows Elder Michaux broadcasting a sermon on WJSV Radio.

3. **Mary Michaux.** This photograph appeared with Mrs. Michaux's column in the Church of God newsletter.

4. **A Baptizing on the Potomac River.** This photograph shows the candidates, choir, and two ministers who will assist Michaux in the baptismal ritual, on a barge in the river. Shores are crowded with church members and other spectators. Scurlock photo, September 3, 1933.

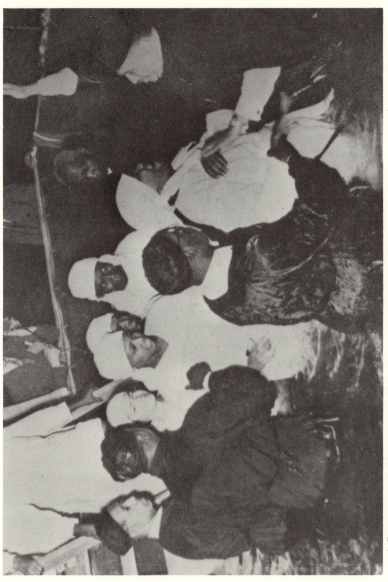

5. **A Baptizing in Griffith Stadium.** This photograph shows Elder Michaux baptizing converts in a pool in Griffith Stadium in Washington, D.C. Photo taken in about 1939.

6. **Michaux Preaching Outdoors.** This photograph shows Michaux preaching at an open air meeting in Hanover, Pennsylvania.

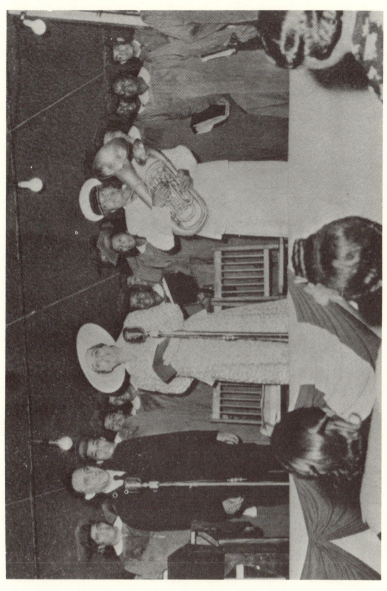

7. **The Michauxs and Choir in Gospel Tent Meeting.** This photograph shows Elder and Mrs. Michaux and a choir in a Philadelphia gospel tent meeting.

8. **Crowds at Gospel Tent Meeting.** This photograph shows a crowded gospel tent meeting in Philadelphia on August 18, 1940. Stanlee photo.

9. **The Cross Choir.** This photograph shows the famous Cross Choir beneath the Lincoln statue in Convention Hall, Philadelphia, during the Seventy-Fifth Anniversary of the Thirteenth Amendment, September 27, 1939.

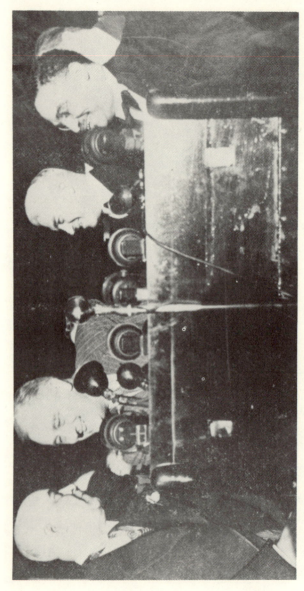

10. **Michaux and President Franklin Roosevelt.** This photograph shows Elder Michaux in a public ceremony with President Franklin Roosevelt.

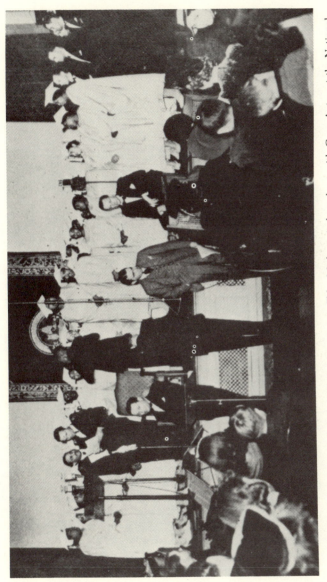

11. **Michaux with Eleanor Roosevelt and Gene Autry.** Elder Michaux in broadcast with Gene Autry at the National Press Club auditorium. Eleanor Roosevelt is seated at the left.

12. **Michaux's Home for Evicted Families.** This photograph shows a view of Michaux's home for evicted families located on southwest corner of Seventh and T streets, NW, Washington, D.C.

13. **The Happy News Café.** This photograph shows the Happy News Café on
Seventh Street in Washington, D.C.

14. **Anniversary Celebration of "Good-Will Tour" to Haiti.** This photograph shows guests at a banquet held in Philadelphia in 1938 to celebrate the first anniversary of the goodwill tour to Haiti.

15. **Michaux with American Indians**. This photograph shows Michaux with a group of American Indians who visited the Church of God.

16. **Michaux in Presidential Victory Parade.** This photograph shows Elder Michaux celebrating Harry Truman's 1948 election during the Democratic Party's victory parade in Washington, D.C.

100

5

"Ain't Got Time to Sin"

Although Michaux no longer received the recognition he thought due him after the late 1930s, he did not lack attention from members. Most of them joined the church prior to 1940, and the Elder anxiously guarded this virtually stabilized group and their offspring. He resorted to various tactics while trying to mold these "peculiar people," as Michaux often called them, into a loyal unit. Toward this effort he created plentiful church activities. This was standard practice in Holiness churches and one conventionally recognized by pastors and other leaders as useful in unifying members.

Because habitual church attendance is of primary importance in acquiring and maintaining unity, Michaux made regular attendance mandatory for those who wanted to keep their membership and position. Members helped enforce the regulation. Therefore, slothful ones risked being detected quickly. Church doors opened at least two times a day, more often on Sundays, usually seven days a week. Whenever a member was slack in attendance, without acceptable excuse, others gave him/her the cold-shoulder. They barely spoke to that person and did not include her/him when planning church affairs. Besides the slothful one frequently was "preached at" from the pulpit by one of the local elders. It was agreed generally among the members that those who did not choose to be in constant assembly with the saints were weak and most susceptible to violating church doctrine, or sinning. One person's sins brought reproach on the whole church. For that reason, members believed watchdog operation was necessary to protect the church's image. After a sinful member was detected, that member was purged.

Members were so busy attending church that they hardly had time for outside interests other than regular employment. They did not belong to clubs, fraternal, or civic organizations to anyone's knowledge. One Washingtonian made perceptive comment on the busy schedule when he saw a choir rehearsal end in the early hours of morning. The man quipped, "Michaux say y'all live a life above sin. Much as he keep y'all in church, you don't have time to sin."[1] Most people familiar with that church, including members, thought the same.

On Monday nights, members gave account of their attendance and support to the church during group meeting when they reported to group leaders. Each group leader was responsible for reporting on activity and inactivity of the fifteen or so members assigned to him/her upon joining the church. Group leaders reported offerings paid, services attended, visitations to the sick and home-bound, work done to help the church advance, such as the amount of *Happy News* sold or paid for. Every group meeting opened with the reading of Mal. 3:8-10, which begins: "Will a man rob God? Yet ye have robbed me. But ye say, wherein have we robbed thee? In tithes and offerings." This was the weekly reminder that tithing and giving to the church are acts of worship performed on the basis of one's conscience but judged ultimately by God. When tithing, members were reminded that this act of worship required of them 10 percent of all monies received—whether from wages, gifts, dividends, or interests. Not to offer the full tithe was to cheat God since no one could know what another member's tithe should be. The group meeting, then, was similar to the Methodist class system in purpose and organization.

A routine week offered this regimen of services: daily noon prayer, except on Sundays; evening worship, from 8:00 until around 10:30, except on Saturday; Sunday morning prayer at 5:30; Sunday School, from 9:45 to 11:30; Sunday noon worship; Young People's Sunday Union at 5:30 P.M.; and the children's Sunshine Band which met on a weekday after school.

The order of worship was regulated so that opening hymn was followed by prayer, a selection by the choir, reading of the scripture, testimonies, the sermon, collection of offerings, announcements, and benediction. Only Michaux or his wife could change the order of worship services. The order of services other than regular worship was tailored to the purpose of that particular assembly.

Testifying was the highpoint of worship unless the Elder or another dynamic preacher was present. Whenever the Spirit was running high among them, members literally ran to get into church before testimonies began. They especially were anxious to hear those of more senior members who talked about the "goodness of God" as if it were something physically palatable that could be feasted upon and savored. These members seemed to want everybody else to feel God's presence as intensely as they did. It was a special treat to hear one brother testify because he stood tall, threw his head back, closed his eyes and sang, "Jesus, Savior, Pilot Me," making a person nearly flinch at suddenly, though vicariously, coming upon "hiding rocks" and "treacherous shoals" of life. [2]

The Holy Spirit ran high, much as it was expected to, every three months during the ten-day revival for members. The Elder first started this revival in 1928, when a crisis occurred in the church in Newport News. After he began traveling to other cities, young adults, who lived together in the church home, became more relaxed around each other, disregarding the sibling relationship that Michaux tried to establish among them. As a result, they succumbed to physical attractions and began to have sexual intercourse with each other's spouses. One of these was a popular deacon. When word of this situation reached Michaux, he rushed back to Newport News and called a ten-day "solemn assembly" of fasting and praying. Although several marriages were permanently disrupted, those involved seemed contrite, and the Elder declared the ten-day meeting successful. He thought it so successful, in fact, that he scheduled periods of fasting and praying for four times a year—on the first Fridays of January, April, July, and October.[3]

During the ten days, members sought after the Holy Spirit. It could be showered upon them at any time and in any place—at home, on the job, on the bus, in church. Those who had been filled prayed for increased spiritual strength, sometimes calling for a "double portion of the Holy Spirit."[4] These members already claimed conversion, yet "being filled with the Holy Spirit" approximated a conversion experience according to testimonies. An explanation of how one in the Church of God reacted to the "downpouring" cannot be expressed better than William James' descriptions on conversion experiences in *Varieties of Religion*. He gives these accounts from testimonies:

> I had been clearly converted twenty-three years before, or rather reclaimed. My experience in regeneration was then clear and spiritual, and I had not backslidden. But I experienced entire sanctification on the 15th day of March, 1893, about eleven o'clock in the morning. The particular accompaniments of the experience were entirely unexpected. I was quietly sitting at home singing selections out of Pentecostal hymns. Suddenly there seemed to be a something sweeping into me and inflating my entire being—such a sensation as I had never experienced before. When this experience came, I seemed to be conducted around a large, capacious, well-lighted room. As I walked with my invisible conductor and looked around, a clear thought was coined in my mind, "They are not here, they are gone." As soon as the thought was definitely formed in my mind, though no word was spoken, the Holy Spirit impressed me that I was surveying my own soul. Then, for the first time in all my life, did I know that I was cleansed from all sin, and filled with the fullness of God.

Another convert testified:

> One Sunday night, I resolved that when I got home to the ranch where I was working, I would offer myself with my faculties and all to God to be used only by and for him. . . . I remember holding out my hands to God and telling him they should work for him, my feet walk for him, my tongue speak for him, . . . if he would only use me as his instrument and give me a satisfying experience—when suddenly

the darkness of the night seemed lit up—I felt, realized, knew that
God heard and answered my prayer. Deep happiness came over me;
I felt I was accepted into the inner circle of God's loved ones.[5]

These late nineteenth century conversion experiences easily could
have come from members of the Church of God as they told how
the Holy Spirit swept over and affected them. They said they remembered when and where they were filled and what they were
doing at that time. Some said they had given up, after having diligently fasted, prayed, and lived as perfectly as possible, when un-
expectedly God baptized them with the Holy Spirit. They spoke
of brightness, lightness, newness and, caught up in the euphoria,
women sometimes took off false hair, saying they wanted nothing
about them to be false. After this spiritual catharsis, members said
they knew God had saved them to life eternal. As James expressed
it, they had reached the "state of assurance." The Holy Spirit man-
ifested itself thereafter in an attitude of holiness. Those who claimed
it tried to live up to standards of "sainthood" as Michaux interpreted
it from the Bible. In the Church of God, loyalty to the church and
its standards followed from being filled with the Holy Spirit.

The regular schedule of services continued during the ten-day
fast except that the Thursday night Purity Club was preempted
for worship, and members gathered to worship on Saturday night
also. Each service ended with congregational prayer rather than
benediction because the sanctity of worship was continuous until
the series ended. These ten-day revivals culminated on the tenth
evening, a Sunday, in all-night prayer meeting, which lasted from
midnight to 5:00 A.M. All-night prayer meetings moved swiftly
because prayer was interspersed with communion, foot-washing,
testimony, shouting, singing, and sermonettes.[6]

Purity Club was the only service displaced by the ten-day revival.
As the only service specifically for young people, it was considered
least in importance to the general membership and leadership. Michaux rarely visited Purity Club, leaving it to his wife's charge
since she had shown an interest in working with young people.
In the 1920s and 1930s, Mrs. Michaux took youths to activities
at Hampton Institute and provided other "proper" entertainment
for them. She attended Purity Club often and her contribution

primarily was by illustrations brought in to show the young saints how to and how not to dress and behave. That was her best opportunity also to exhort young girls to be virtuous, to be as she euphemistically termed it, "a peach out of reach!" In her absence and from the 1930s on, energetic women conducted Purity Club. High points for the youth were the marching drills and the timed Bible Sword Drill. In this latter activity, whoever "cut" to the called-out scripture first won a prize, usually a beautiful Bible, curio, wallet, but the award went to the person who won four or five consecutive weeks. A repast followed the service. Aside from Bible study, marching and other drills and talent programs, Purity Club was a time, like Sunday Evening Union, when boys and girls could meet and talk without the watchful eyes of their parents before the service began, before it ended, or during repast. As a result, youth attendance was high at Purity Club and Sunday Evening Union, and parents rarely attended either. When church leaders, however, did not adapt this service to meet changing needs of their more worldly-involved and wise youth, attendance dwindled and Purity Club struggled to maintain its viability after the late 1950s.

Michaux believed that if he could hold members' interest, he could better insure loyalty. Therefore, he scheduled special events and programs, some of which coincided with national holidays. At those times, members traveled to the several churches for celebration. During these gatherings, they visited in each other's homes, feasted home-style in the host church's dining hall, and attended a religious pageant or program performed by representatives of the various churches. Such was the order of events on New Year's Day in Philadelphia, on Founder's Day in Washington, Mother's Day in New York City, Father's Day in Baltimore, Michaux's birthday in Washington, and Thanksgiving Day in Newport News. The National Memorial beachfront in Jamestown was the center of activity on the Fourth of July to celebrate Mrs. Michaux's birthday and on Easter Monday when festivities included an egg roll and fish fry. Fish fries were held at Pinkey's Beach in Newport News until the mid-1960s, when crowds of strong young men who were not members of the church became unmanageable for the aging Elder. The year's high point always was the Annual Baptizing in Washington.[7]

Via these special events, Michaux hoped to knit together the widely separated churches, so he permitted members to suggest ideas for these occasions. The idea for an annual Founder's Day, for example, originated with a sister in Washington, and that day was celebrated for the first time in 1949, with Mrs. Eleanor Roosevelt as special guest.[8] Mother's and Father's Day celebrations also were created by members, and they were instituted during the 1950s and 1960s, respectively. On those days, members who were mothers and fathers sometimes received recognition, such as being the eldest or the one with the most children. These "parent" days actually resembled additional opportunities to honor the founders although they did not originate with that intention.[9]

An addition to these were unscheduled funerals and weddings. The best account of these in the Church of God was in the movie "We've Come A Long, Long Way." Funerals had less pageantry than those black ones stereotyped in literature and video media. Michaux did not preach about the dead, rather he directed sermons to relatives and friends of the deceased, calling them to repentance. He emphasized rejoicing over the death of a saint. Fraternal Orders did not turn out at Church of God funerals since members had no active affiliation in them, and the general rule-of-thumb was that nonmembers could not be funeralized there. Weddings presented "low church" ceremony and spectacular.

To perform adequately the myriad duties incidental to church services, programs, and special activities, numerous organizations and groups formed. In a manner traditionally characteristic of black churches, some of Michaux's members held a "place" in several groups and organizations.[10] The unlettered and the untrained, as well as those with education and formal training, had opportunity to serve and to develop talents.[11] In the black church maids, janitors, and hotel porters could become deacons, preachers, trustees, soloists, ushers, and Sunday School teachers. Although this avenue to development of talent and leadership was not exclusively the black church's, traditionally it was through this medium that black folk received recognition and status often denied them outside the church community.[12]

Exhibiting the need for recognition and the desire to display talents, men and women, boys and girls in the several Churches of God volunteered to join choirs, orchestras, program committees, usher boards, sewing and cooking circles, and management and office staffs. Many received on-the-job training while serving. Young men, for example, often volunteered to work with skilled technicians on microphones, or taping and photographic equipment to learn that trade while serving the church. Drama directors selected participants for plays and programs according to speaking, singing, and acting talents, and that group of performers stabilized. All were without special training, but they got ideas about how to direct or perform from reading and attending plays and programs, where permissible. Some youngsters joined the junior choir and usher board, and local deacons, with tacit approval of elders, appointed several young men to the nonconsequential board of junior deacons. Adults sometimes earned their daily livelihood at tasks they volunteered to perform for the church, especially if they were cooks, seamstresses, photographers, teachers, secretaries, or electricians. Despite free time and services given, there still was always more to be done at church than there were members with interest, time, and energy to spare.

Even though the Elder concentrated on keeping members busy, he also made a bid to attract the public to services. Each summer he held ten-day, soul-winning, old camp ground revivals. In major cities from Virginia to New York, he pitched a huge tent on a large vacant lot and proclaimed the Gospel. Although these summer evening services were held occasionally in church edifices, the tent was Michaux's favorite revival arena.[13]

Decor of the tent was in traditional camp-meeting style. A raised pulpit was decorated with red, white, and blue bunting. Wooden folding chairs stood in neat rows on sawdust or on sand. Microphones loomed about the pulpit, and loudspeakers, perched outside the tent, beamed the message to passers-by. Michaux, a masterful revivalist, was favorably compared to famous evangelists such as Billy Sunday, I. D. Sankey, Dwight Moody. Like them, he knew the value of music to enliven services and to attract attention of the public. Hence, he used music lavishly, interspersing gospel singing throughout each service. Mrs. Michaux, with her golden, soprano voice, led the congregation and choir in songfest from song cards.[14] The Elder preached sermons with catchy titles like "Where did the Devil come from?" "Where is the Devil?" "Where is Hell?" "Where is Heaven?" "Signs of the End of the World," "Are you a member of a church? If so what profit is it to you?" Michaux also billed side attractions. There were special choirs from his churches in other cities, or features such as a mummified imp in glass coffin. This imp allegedly was a "child" of the Devil.[15]

After 1940, Michaux incurred difficulties in erecting tents since some communities did not take kindly to having gospel festivity, with large crowds, in their midst. Residents of Harlem's prestigious Sugar Hill, for example, opposed a tent meeting on one occasion but were unsuccessful in obtaining a court injunction to prohibit it.[16] Erecting tents became increasingly difficult for Michaux as local officials tightened fire and other safety regulations. From year to year, the Elder battled against rising costs and community resistance to meet regulations and to obtain a permit before scheduled openings. In 1960, he opened his Richmond meeting without a permit and was summoned to court.[17] He really struggled to keep his favorite evangelistic medium alive and managed to hold tent meetings, at least intermittently, until a year or two before his death, when his own failing health was the obstacle.[18]

The enterprising Michaux also held open-air, or block revivals, instituting them where local regulations made it difficult or inconvenient to erect a tent. Block meetings were on vacant lots, with poles throughout, giving the impression that he intended to use them for a tent. The area was wired for lighting, for an amplifying system, and was replete with folding chairs, and pulpit.[19]

Another genre of open air services that Michaux held was the street meeting. Actually it served as advertisement for revivals. Michaux arranged them for early evening, just before regularly scheduled services, in an effort to reach people leaving work. A street meeting, per se, was brief. The Elder, or one of his local elders, preached soapbox style and invited passers-by to the revival. They, with the group that accompanied them, formed a procession and sang as they marched to the church, tent, or block setting, hoping people heard and would follow.[20]

Advertisement did not end there. Members distributed professionally printed handbills to neighbors, relatives, coworkers, and
business proprietors.[21] The church placed ads in newspapers, and
it was not unusual to see automobiles or trucks outfitted with loudspeakers and placards, heralding the coming of the revival.[22] One
might also be jolted upon seeing a man dressed to portray the Devil,
perched atop a vehicle with a snake, whose body, Michaux said,
housed the Devil's spirit, to herald the coming "war on the Devil."[23]
The most effective advertisement was the people who annually
attended and invited neighbors, friends, and relatives to accompany
them to a festive, out-door service, on a hot summer night.

For years Michaux's meetings attracted huge crowds. His devoted
supporters were members, and they brought coworkers, relatives,
neighbors, and employers. Curious passers-by frequently stopped
and listened. The Elder sent special invitations to other local congregations whose doctrinal beliefs were similar to his church's,
as for example, the Saint Timothy Church in Newport News. These
congregations attended in a body with their pastor, sometimes invited by Michaux to give invocation and benediction. Night after night,
there was standing room only. Hundreds crowded under the tent
while others pressed tightly around the outside, straining to hear
every word and to see every move.[24]

The most enticing church event was the Annual Baptizing. On
that occasion, new converts and other members, who had not been
baptized and those who wanted to be baptized again, received that
rite en masse. More than a baptismal ritual, though the baptizing
was a spectacular production. It exhibited the church's viability
and Michaux's large following. This occasion gave him an opportunity to welcome all Americans to his church and to display the
fact that he, too, was an American, as he gave the event a patriotic
air. Red, white, and blue bunting covered the baptismal tank and
the pulpit, and the crowds sang "God Bless America." Excitement and
pageantry of this day's activities alone did much to inspire those
who joined recently to stay in the church.[25]

Before Michaux went to Washington, his baptizings were quiet
religious sacraments, without fanfare, administered on beachfronts
in Newport News and Hampton. When he acquired radio fame and
a big following in Washington, the Elder moved this event to the

Potomac River. There a steamer carried him, his wife, and other elders, musicians, and candidates to a barge from which the actual baptizings were conducted. Huge crowds lined the bank to observe.[26] After 1938, Michaux baptized from Griffith Stadium in Washington during August or September until that baseball relic closed in 1961. From that year on, he held baptizings in the Coliseum and other locations around the city.[27]

About one month prior to the baptizing, local deacons polled congregations in their respective churches for names of candidates. Interested ones, from age seven to seventy, received instructions on what to wear and where to report once they arrived in Washington. All wore white cotton gowns, white, rubber-bottom shoes, and wrapped white towels around their heads. There was no charge or request of donation for baptism.

The ritual began when candidates, varying from 75 to 400 in number, signaled by Michaux's entrance into the pool, started singing "Lead me to the water to be baptized," as they marched forward. Michaux baptized them "in the name of the Father, of the Son, and of the Holy Ghost" in a four-foot canvas pool filled with water by the fire department. He was assisted by two or three of his ministers who, like him, dressed in black gowns, black hip boots, and black skull caps.[28]

An occasional, overjoyed candidate splashed around in the pool. Dollard, and later Herskovits, concluded that Negro baptizings were of African derivation or orientation because of spirit possession following immersion. Although the Yoruba and Ashanti are associated with water ritual, in Dahomey where river cults exist, worshippers are drawn to the water and upon touching it are possessed with the spirit. Emphasis in these cults is on streams rather than a pool of drawn water. In this respect Michaux's baptizings did not bear kinship to African river cults after he stopped baptizing in natural streams if they ever really did. These authors also claim that black Americans generally are attracted to Baptist churches because they practice baptism by immersion. They surmised that black Baptists relate to that ritual naturally because of their African river cult ancestry.[29] Tradition and ancestry may well have figured in Michaux's adoption of immersion, but it was handed down by way of the Baptist and Holiness churches to him. Unlike them, though, he added innovation to the ritual by conducting mass, annual baptizings. Clergy in his previous church affiliations baptized on an individual and small group scale, and they baptized several times a year as converts joined their churches.

The baptismal ritual was the culmination of the evening service which featured the famous 156 voice Cross Choir and a pageant. The Cross Choir was so named because it sat in the form of a cross and dressed in white satin robes and skull caps. Both male and female, young and old came to perform in the choir from the several churches.

After the Michauxs and their special guests made their entrance onto the ball park field, the choir marched in to the tune of "Hear the Tramp, Tramp, Tramp of the Army"; this was played by the band. Choir members carried deftly concealed miniature flags of all nations, crowns, and other accoutrements. Their performance was like that of a drill team. Appointed ones moved to form letters as their director, Michaux or someone whom he designated, also dressed in white, cued them. The Cross Choir performed with precision, thrilling the thousands who packed the stadium.[30]

Baptismal pageants were spectacular portrayals of scenes from the Bible with accompanying fireworks. Drama and fireworks splashed together in colorful combination. The evening when the Second Coming of Christ was portrayed in Griffith Stadium is an example. "From behind a 40 x 50 foot cloud . . . a figure [one of the Elder's parishioners] representing Christ emerged and descended as the dead . . . [burst forth from graves] in the center field bleachers. Chorus and congregation [swayed and] sang, 'There'll be shouting on the hills of glory.' "[31] Another memorable pageant illustrated the "Broken heart of Christ." An electric, bleeding heart spilled crimson fluid on twelve penitent females while the Cross Choir sang, 'There is a fountain filled with blood, drawn from Emmanuel's vein."[32] The enthusiastic crowds were entertained from time to time with portrayals of the devil's funeral and the Ascension of Christ.[33]

The merging of a vast display of pageantry, fireworks, and the ritual of baptism made the Annual Baptizing unique in American church history. It was here that Michaux most skillfully displayed his talents for showmanship and innovation.

The church advertised Annual Baptizings widely. Major newspapers and businesses, in cities across the Church of God's field, cooperated in the advertising drive. Papers carried ads, pointing out special events to take place, as for instance those of the then forthcoming 1934 Baptizing where the "Happy Am I" film would be shown. In 1949, Michaux advertised that Sergeant Hendrix, who had fallen one hundred feet from an airplane and survived, would attend the baptizing. He billed Hendrix as a "Miracle Man" like Truman who miraculously won the presidential election in 1948. The upcoming 1950 baptizing was headlined: "Cotton-clad Candidates for World's Biggest Baptism Will Be Buried in the Jordan's Water." The article informed readers that Michaux shipped in twelve barrels of Jordan River water and that the filling of them was certified by a Scottish Presbyterian missionary in Israel. As further inducement, the article continued by pointing out that a lucky 1,000 people would receive vials of the water during the baptizing.[34]

There were other ingenious methods of advertising. Each baptizing, for example, was preceded with three to four weeks of Sunday evening services in the ball park. Early on the day of the big event, a parade-sightseeing-advertising tour of Washington took place. Buses and cars with placards, floats, bands, and choirs formed contingents of the parade to remind interested Washingtonians that the day for the baptizing had arrived.[35]

Thousands attended each year. Church officials estimated attendance by counting seats, corroborating the count with ticket receipts. In 1932 a racial breakdown appeared: officials estimated that 50.3 percent blacks, 48.1 percent whites, and 1.3 percent others attended the baptizing that year.[36] Heavy attendance attracted press scrutiny, and newspapers and magazines printed estimated attendance: "20,000 Applaud As Elder Michaux Baptizes," "15,000 Sing Old Hymns at Stadium," "20,000 Witness Baptism in River of Jordan Water," "19,000 See Religious Portrayal," "23,000 See Elder Michaux Baptize."[37] Estimates went as high as 40,000 for a single night.[38]

Besides members Michaux usually could count on two or three celebrities. Students and faculty from Howard University often attended not only for entertainment but also to gather research data.

After the 1940s, their attendance was less steady.[39] The most avid
and loyal fans were members. They returned year after year, often
traveling long distances to participate in the event-filled day. Local
church officials arranged for mass transportation to encourage
attendance. In 1948 a train excursion of twelve coaches took members and friends from the Tidewater area to Washington. Folk sometimes went in automobiles, the church's old double-decker bus,
"Happy," or on Greyhound and Trailway buses. One year a con-
voy of twelve Greyhound buses breezed along the highway to
Washington from Newport News, while several others carried the
loyal and the curious from New York, Philadelphia, and
Baltimore.[40]

A black journalist, evaluating the legendary and historical significance of Annual Baptizings, observed that "it was with spectacular
annual ball park baptismals, in Washington's old Griffith Stadium,
that Elder Michaux became a legend."[41] One reporter with the *Washington Post* noted, "Michaux . . . made headlines for many feats, but
the 'Happy Am I' preacher probably will be remembered longest for
his ball park meetings, religious extravaganzas that qualify him as
a great showman."[42] On the other hand, the drama and extravaganza
caused some contemporaries to conclude that Michaux was no
example of intelligence, but was only a showman and a joke in
religious circles.[43] There was the added comment by others that
several successful and respected preachers, especially evangelists,
intuitively are showmen, trying to attract attention of masses.
Whether Michaux created the Annual Baptizing as one of many
activities designed to hold members' and followers' attention, or to
publicize the Church of God, or to flaunt his popularity before
people of influence, he manipulated this ingenious design toward
accomplishing all of these ends.

The regimen of activity devised under Michaux kept members
preoccupied as well as busy. Preoccupation, though, does not insure
commitment to whatever is occupying one. Therefore, initially
appealing programs eventually lose magnetism if they are not made
to seem continuously vital to participants' psychological well-being.
Because Michaux understood this he tried to convince members
that if they left the Church of God their existence outside would be
despairing.

6

To Control a "Holy" People

Since Michaux did not presume that just keeping members busy was adequate strategy for maintaining their loyalty, he also applied psychological controls. Mainly he was anxious to entrench authority. Therefore, he magnified the importance of his leadership to the Church of God. Foremost in the formula for entrenching authority was the Elder's insistence on respect for leadership. Statements to this effect, such as the one below, were direct. "Any intelligent person," he counseled assembled deacons and elders,

> knows that you must respect your leader. . . . Nothing but a lot of ignoramuses disrespect leadership. When intelligent people come together with a mind to accomplish something, the first thing they do is to elect a leader. And whatever the leader says is to be done they do. . . . And if they don't like the leader they get rid of him. But you can't get rid of a leader as long as he follows the standard of the organization.[1]

Such sweeping statements undoubtedly raised unasked questions in the minds of those assembled. Obviously Michaux was reminding them to respect him. But he was not elected or called by the membership, rather the church had begun under him, and he invited folk to join with him. Had he confused authoritarian privileges inherent in the founder-leader type situation with those where leader was not founder? Could anyone besides him influence decision-making? If they tired of his leadership, could the congregation get rid of him? Didn't he set standards against which he would be measured? Did Michaux use the word respect when he meant deference? Anyone pondering such questions would find answers in time.

Meanwhile the Elder masked his implied requests for deference from members by assuming an egalitarian air. He, in fact, endeared himself to members by proclaiming high regard for them. He often said, for example, "Now precious ones, . . . I am always honored when I find myself in the midst of holy brethren, that is a class that has out-classed the world."[2] When moving behind the pulpit, he often shaded his eyes and looked over his audience, asking about faithful and elderly members who were absent.[3] Sometimes he gave special greeting to those whom he had missed on previous trips to that church or who had recently recovered from serious illness or problems. After service, he moved among the congregation, speaking to and shaking hands with first one and then another member. He paused to listen as they burdened him with their individual financial problems, illnesses, and family crises.

As he circulated among them, members were impressed that Michaux seemed unassuming and humble, but also like an inscrutable prophet. Although most members thought he was of patrician stature because of his avowed influence with persons of national or local importance, they delighted in hearing him deny that he felt like a "big shot." He did so at the end of an annual Easter fish fry for example. On that occasion, he said:

> I was . . . glad to be . . . giving those folks that fish and bread even
> though they attacked me, [were] up on top of me, grabbing me and
> kicking me. . . . I didn't get mad because they acted as they did. I
> was their servant. I am not interested in being a big shot like [Bishop]
> Grace. If he were down there, his followers would have to take him
> up on their shoulders and carry him around.[4]

Members were satisfied to believe they had surrendered themselves into the charge of an unobtrusive, yet prominent figure.

Their esteem for Michaux increased with their belief that he was an inscrutable prophet, for they tested the validity of his predictions over an extended period of time.[5] He rarely, and to much effect, tapped into that aspect of their faith in him to keep them subdued. He occasionally pronounced predictions to intimidate, as for example, the night he "prophesied" that a deacon who had just "disrespected" leadership would see his children suffer. The Elder had asked that deacon, who was financially comfortable, to give $50 in collection. The man gave $5 instead, and Michaux, visibly annoyed, declared, "He can take care of himself, but he can't take care of his children." Many, who heard, even the two daughters, believed that declaration was a curse. Consequently, when the elder daughter's husband beat her and sent her home to her parents, that was no more than was expected based upon their interpretation of Michaux's "prophecy."[6] Members magnified the importance of prophecies such as that one, for they believed any predictions the Elder made would materialize. Therefore, they did not quibble over their vagueness nor over the outcome of situations about which he prophesied. Add to this acceptance and faith the fact that Michaux said he could discern spirits, and one begins to realize how intimidating his fearsome tactics were to those who did not reason that all effective leaders discern spirits.

Members thought Michaux and his wife were special people sent to them, a lowly folk, by God, and they displayed their feelings by rising to honor them when they entered church. Careful not to accept honor immodestly, the Elder reminded members whom they should reverence, saying: "When you rise to honor me, I kneel to honor God."[7] In keeping with this articulated attitude, Michaux discouraged charismatic demonstrations directed toward him. He gave an example of the kind of exhibition he would not tolerate:

One day while preaching . . . a young lady, fairly decent in her appearance, came up as we were about to dismiss and . . . asked me to pray for her baby. And when I bowed over her to pray for the child [,] I noticed that although she was not drunk, she had the smell of whiskey on her breath. So I asked her just what was wrong with her baby. And while she was talking [,] I notice[d] her make a little

quick move. . . . Nevertheless, I laid my hand on her. . . . And as
I began to pray[,] she dropped the baby and fell sprawling on the
floor, shivering and kicking, . . . She was carrying on so that I told
the brothers to put her on the bench. I began to preach about how
the devil had thrown her down and made her drop her child. . . . I
was telling the saints how the devil was in a man's son and how the
devil had thrown this man down on the ground and even in[to] the
fire but that the disciples could not heal this man or even make the
devil come out of the man.

Michaux continued further, explaining that only Jesus had power
to cast the devil out of the man and that the woman wanted to make
him think he, too, had such power.

When she came back up and stood before me, . . . she said . . .
"When you laid your hand upon me to pray, something struck me on
the crown of my head and went all through me. You are wonderful."
But I knew . . . that was the devil trying to praise me and at the same
time deceive me by making me think . . . I knocked her out with my
power. . . . Anybody you see being knocked out when somebody is
praying for them, the devil is using that person. [8]

Pentecostals always were located up the street and around the corner
from Michaux's churches. They believed God impressed those that
were to be blessed by causing them to fall out when the preacher
touched and prayed for them. In contrast to that doctrine, Michaux
did not believe God ever caused anyone to be knocked out. No
member would dare fall out for fear of being reprimanded before
the congregation and ostracized by members.

Likewise, because he feared people would be confused about the
source of healing power, Michaux would not accept the mantle
of faith healer. After 1933, he would not pray in large gatherings
for someone with an obviously disabling ailment to be healed. During
that year's baptizing, a sixty-year old paraplegic whom he had
invited was "on stage" to be healed. The Elder prayed and immersed
her in the Potomac River seven times, and she still was paralyzed.
Imagine his chagrin when newspapers carried that story of failure
in the next day's headline. From that day, he made no fanfare about

praying for people to be healed. He prayed for ailing members, however, and suggested remedies. One member said she was dead, heard the Elder call her and revived. Another woman told the congregation that Michaux advised her to anoint her head with Listerine after X-rays showed a tumor inside her skull. She ecstatically said the tumor disappeared after she tried the Listerine. Among other remedies suggested by Michaux was one for diabetes. He advised those with this ailment to eat a mixture of raw vegetables with meals but without bread for a prescribed number of days. He said he had tried it and his sugar count was lowered. If as diabetics, they craved sweets, the Elder told members to eat a spoonful of ice cream, follow with an eight ounce glass of water, then eat another spoonful of ice cream. They had tasted ice cream and felt full, he said. Those who tried that treatment said they found it useful in controlling their diabetes while satisfying their taste. All of this activity concerning healing and prescribing remedies took place inside the safety of the congregation. Michaux would not be blamed if a prayer for healing was not answered or a remedy failed, for members believed God was the source of all cures and would restore health according to Divine will. But never again, after the 1933 fiasco, did Michaux publicly pray for anyone's healing.[9]

Not all members were deceived by Michaux's mask of unassumingness and unobtrusiveness in his presentation of himself as leader. Knowing he also could be tough and unyielding, even cutting in his reprimands, they stayed on guard. One area in which he was inflexible was that of requiring obedience. He demanded complete obedience to directives and emphasized consequences of disobedience, especially of disobedience to him as God's prophet. Using the example of Adam and Eve, he said,

The price for disobedience is . . . annihilation, extermination . . . extinction. . . . Adam, the first disobedient man [,] brought the sentence of death upon all men. There must be obedience to the letter. Obey the prophet! When the word goes out, no matter what the cost may seem to be to you, be ready to do it or die. . . . Forsaking wife, land, property, children . . . leaving everything to obey the command of the prophet.[10]

Blind obedience, the Elder said, would make the church more than a "sect, another little gang in a storefront, another little shouting, noisy, fuss-making group of folks."[11] Michaux was savvy. He realized his members felt compelled to be obedient. Obedience to him satisfied their inner need to surrender themselves to a higher power which Michaux represented to them.

There were several specific directives that Michaux issued to govern members' conduct, as for example those pertaining to marriage and divorce. Members were forbidden to marry nonmembers, and divorce was sanctioned only on grounds of adultery.[12] Trying to lessen the need or desire to sue for divorce, Michaux talked to members about the kind of relationship he thought properly should exist between a husband and wife. He gave this instruction during one assembly:

> You want a wife no other man can touch. The Lord says you got to sanctify her to yourself, take her from . . . everybody else and let her be one with you. When you marry a woman, if you don't have nothing but a box to carry her into, move in the box. Some folks let others stay in their home; that's all right if you can take it, but you're going to have trouble. . . . Men [ought] to love their wives as their own bodies. He that loveth his wife loveth himself. For no man ever yet hated his own flesh. . . . No misgivings, no let-up, not just taking things for granted after you're married. Before you married it was all honey pie this and darling that and sweetheart the other. But just as soon as the honey-moon was over, you did everything else but nourished, cherished, or petted her. Brother, you've got it to do.[13]

He also instructed members on the kind of relationship he thought should exist between parents and children to insure family harmony. Mainly he cautioned parents not to allow their children, through disobedience, to bring "reproach on [the] family's name." Michaux warned that a disobedient spirit could spread from one child to another and explained how a disobedient spirit could be identified. Daughters who were pregnant and unmarried, or who had children out of wedlock, were disobedient to the church tenet that men and women should remain chaste until married. Sons who committed misdemeanors and felonies blatantly violated church as well as civil law. To teach malefactors a lesson and to impress upon their siblings undesirable consequences of such behavior Michaux urged parents to do the following: Put unwed daughters who are pregnant out; visit imprisoned sons but do not pay bail or fines for them. The worst of these offences was pregnancy before marriage; at least treatment accorded these unfortunate ones seemed to indicate this.

Whenever an unmarried teenager became pregnant, she was punished severely. First she was "put out of the church." Next, she was put out of her parents' home and had to take shelter in homes of nonchurch family or friends if both parents were members in the Church of God. These girls felt the displacement from home acutely and often sneaked to their mothers to be assured that they still were loved. Fathers usually took a harder line than mothers because as males they often held positions of relative authority in church and felt their places threatened by the domestic situation. Privately, however, some fathers longed to comfort their daughters. One, a preacher, told friends years later how he put his daughter out because the Elder said he should. During her pregnancy, though, he turned his head while she sneaked home to her mother for food and comfort. Homesickness was compounded by ostracism from fellowship with friends since most of them were members of the church and forbidden to associate with the pregnant girl. Moreover, before the 1960s, a girl who was pregnant was put out of school as well unless she ran into enlightened teachers willing to shelter her from discovery by school authorities until the end of the year or as long as possible. Meanwhile the young expectant father was merely silenced in church and was likely to be undisturbed in school. He was encouraged to complete his education and to attend church with family and friends.

Mothers of unmarried, pregnant girls were punished also while fathers usually were not. Michaux's thinking was that mothers are responsible for their daughters' moral training, and where a girl "strayed," her mother had been careless. So the mother was silenced in church, and her church friends shied away from her. Most of these mothers endured their suffering stoically and assured their daughters that they still loved them although they felt disgraced by their condition.

One result of the church's attitude on this matter of unwed mothers was that most of these young women suffered emotional trauma from which they never recovered. Upon rejoining the church, they harbored resentment, against members and the Michauxs, for years. They usually did not stay long in the church after returning. If there was any redeeming value in the face of such negative ramifications, it must have been lodged in the fact that the out-of-wedlock birthrate was virtually negligible in the Church of God. Members considered abortion so murderously sinful that none felt need to dignify the issue with discussion.

These rules and attitudes regarding pregnancy before marriage were strictly enforced until the 1960s with its liberating ideas. It was during the 1960s also that the Michaux's Eskimo girl (see note 10, chap. 1) matured into a fun-loving, hard to control teenager. The aging couple then was mellowed by their confrontations with a teenager, and Mrs. Michaux was sinking into mental lethargy. From that time on, unmarried girls who were pregnant went virtually unnoticed by the Michauxs. Local preachers and deacons did not command authority to force rules upon parents and could only be sure that unwed mothers did not participate in church activities. These girls no longer were put out of their parents' homes, and frequently parents kept the grandchild so the daughter could be free to pursue an education.[14]

Michaux believed judgement begins at the House of God. Therefore, he exhorted members not to take frictions with each other into civil court. "Any matter that comes up must be settled among you and never in a court room among ungodly folks," he admonished. Explaining why, he quoted from I Cor. 6:

> Dare any of you, having a matter against another, go to law before the unjust, and not before the saints? Do ye not know that the saints shall judge the world? And if the world shall be judged by you, are ye unworthy to judge the smallest matters? Know ye not that we shall judge angels? How much more things that pertain to this life?[15]

And he established a biblically-inspired procedure to guide them in placing charges of disobedience or apostacy against each other.

That procedure, taken from Matt. 18, consisted of four basic steps:

1) The eyewitness to the violation was instructed to go privately to the offender to discuss the charge.

2) If the offender did not repent or if he committed the violation a second time, the eyewitness was to take a second member to discuss the charge with the offender.

3) If the offender remained unrepentant, he was then to be taken, by the eyewitness, before the church (actually a body of deacons and elders) which would act as jury and judge.

4) That body of church officials would decide how to punish the offender, basing their decision on the Bible and on Michaux's previous decisions in similar cases. [16]

Rules, directives, and exhortations generated an atmosphere of suspicion and spying among members. Each was an agent who would suppress personal tendencies to commit sin by spying on others. Implicit in this atmosphere of suspicion was the attitude that all members have sin-potential and that each must act as "brother's keeper," either to help others toe the line or to ferret out hypocrites. In this respect, suspicion was a unifying element. "Knowing themselves watched," Eric Hoffer wrote about small social movements, "the faithful strive to escape suspicion by adhering zealously to prescribed behavior and opinion." [17] An occasional "hypocrite" was caught smoking, drinking, or courting someone else's spouse. These detected ones usually left the church of their own accord, or, after being confronted with their wrongdoing, straightened up. Every member was vulnerable, for any one of them could be charged with violations, tried, and punished. Punishment could take several forms—expulsion from the church, demotion from position, and/or silencing.

Unless members adhered to church standards, they were not exhibiting fruits of saintliness, and that meant, according to Michaux's interpretation, they were sinners who would be weeded out. Some felt threatened by the certainty that punishment would come to violators. They were threatened because of their belief that through the fellowship in the Church of God, they had acquired a better life and emotional security. They recalled their former failings and insecurities when facing life alone, and that past seemed cold and dreary. Benefits they derived from membership caused most to dread thoughts of being cast out.[18] Michaux understood how they felt. Therefore, he skillfully whipped them into conformity by applying analogies such as that of a tree limb's demise, when broken away from the trunk, to members' fate if "put out of the church." The Elder would say, we will "cut them off. A limb is not any good if it is off the tree."[19]

Michaux sometimes put a person out of church for breaking rules or lowering standards of the Church of God. He related a case in which the man, a member, appeared to be too intimate with a woman to whom he was not married:

> Brother ——— was speaking to me . . . about Brother ——— in the Church, who was reported to have conducted himself in an unduly familiar way with some woman while sitting around in a car. . . . Now Brother ——— was very upset about this matter and said . . . he didn't want to worry me with it too. I told him that was no worry [,] for any time anybody isn't right . . . *Put Them Out* [sic] and then send for me to come. . . . The rule in this church is whenever you find uncleanness or sin . . . you don't have to wait for the Elder [to put the person out].[20]

The most serious offence was that of trying to divide members or "split the church." Its seriousness was detectable in the tone of Michaux's statement when he expelled two members from church on that account. The Elder remarked,

> We're going to excommunicate Mr. ——— and Mr. ——— . . . as heretics—those who would divide. . . . They [began] to openly rebel against the church and your leaders, . . . going around secretly trying to divide. . . .
>
> Now you watch those who go out from among us. I've seen them go time and time again, but I have yet to see one of them prosper. Satan blinds them![21]

An excommunicated person could be reinstated, depending on how Michaux felt about the person's contrition. If he previously had held any position of authority, and only men were deacons or elders, the returning one could not hold that place again. The reason, according to Michaux, was that the person could not attract converts since the authenticity of his own conversion was questionable after he once had "fallen."[22]

The most frequently applied punishment for infractions was silencing. Under this restriction, a member was not allowed to testify, preach, or otherwise participate in services, except as an observer, for a specified period of time, usually thirty days. A member might be silenced for failing to keep children under control or for having an unmarried, pregnant daughter. A silenced person was shunned by other members although close friends sometimes befriended each other.

Occasionally, and to everybody's dismay, Mrs. Michaux rebuked members. Her scoldings were searing and hysterical. She singled out suspected apostates, or even those who simply annoyed her, for public tongue lashings and prayed that "God [would] burst their heads wide open." She had no compassion for women whose husbands left them and said to one woman, during a church meeting, "If you can't hold on to your husband, don't come crying on my shoulder." She gave shock treatments. At a well-timed moment during tirades, she flicked her nose with her partially-gloved finger and said, "They [hypocrites] stink in God's nostrils." Members generally agreed that the Elder's chastisement and judgement were more civil and palatable than his wife's. Mrs. Michaux stood before the congregation with a microphone to heap abuse upon members, giving men reason to charge her with preaching, since women were forbidden to preach in the Church of God. The Elder defended her by saying she did not preach, she exhorted. She exhorted in preacher style. A deacon read scriptures for her as she called for and commented on them. She talked as long as she cared to, and no one dared interrupt. After she was satisfied that her points had been made sufficiently, Mrs. Michaux signaled that the preacher for the evening could then deliver his sermon. Often, though, deacons said time was already "far spent" and would take up collection and call for benediction. Woe to a local preacher whom she disliked, for she berated him publicly and tried to block his preaching when she was in that city. An example is that of a preacher, of West Indian origins, who said he attended the House of Prayer, founded by Daddy Grace, before joining the Church of God. Mrs. Michaux never forgave him for having been attracted to Daddy Grace first, and the man suffered much abuse from her mouth. She often took the prerogative of a First Lady and requested that the Elder send her one of her favorite preachers whenever she was in another city.[23]

Although his attitude toward serious violations was clear, Michaux was more anxious to maintain church rolls than to lessen them through reckless, punitive measures. He decided that one way of retaining members was to prohibit them from visiting other churches. Therefore, he established this rule: "We don't go into sect churches because they cannot teach us anything good." His definition of a sect church was one which deviated from primal teachings of Jesus as he interpreted them from the New Testament. He discouraged members from attending funerals or weddings of relatives in other churches. So it was not unusual to see members from the Church of God sitting in cars outside the "sect" church, awaiting the rest of the family that was inside celebrating the funeral or wedding. There were members, however, who Michaux thought were devout but inclined to be independent thinkers. They would attend special ceremonies involving family members in other churches with and without the Elder's permission but always with his tacit support. He gave them license because he recognized that they might become disillusioned with his system of control over them.[24]

Michaux expressed concern that no members be lost from church rolls, except through death. Realizing that not all who joined would remain, he tried to change the minds of potential backsliders by frightening them with predictions of doom. Illustrative of this was the following statement:

> When you find yourself saying . . . you are going to get out and go getting mad with something that doesn't suit you, . . . watch out unless you bring your own destruction. There is no need to allow yourself to become angry with the body [church] you are in because if you look back you'll see that if you are anything with God, the body has made you what you are.[25]

Continuing on with this subject, he said, "Now you can leave the truth if you wish[,] but your judgement will go from you, [sic] your last state will be worst [sic] than before you knew God."[26]

These admonitions did not deter those determined to leave the church. Two elderly women left in 1929 because they disapproved of Michaux's purchase of the old Lincoln Theater and were horrified that he would use it as a sanctuary. Couples left in reaction to disciplinary measures. One couple, that was reared in the church, said they reluctantly withdrew membership around 1945 because they grew weary of Mrs. Michaux's humiliating harangues before the congregation. They joined an African Methodist Episcopal congregation.[27] More typically, though, young adults left the church or got themselves "put out" by attending the theater, dances, or by being caught smoking. While they had been reared in the Church of God, they wanted worldly experiences and thought that church's strictures were too confining.[28]

There were officers who helped Michaux with church administration. They were deacons (local overseers who did not preach) and elders (who preached). Deacons presided over services and handled business of the local church, such as collecting offerings and attending to current expenses and other financial obligations. Each church had several deacons, depending on the size of that church's membership, but usually seven. Elders, with the exception of one or two, were not ordained. There was only one ordination ceremony in the church's history, and that had come early in its history. The one or two ordained ones were survivals from that single ordination. Michaux did issue licenses to preachers once a year, making sure that they were limited in functions they could perform. There were limitations in the performance of wedding ceremonies and interment of the dead, but all had opportunity to preach, often weekly, since there were about four ministers per church and services were almost nightly.[29]

Michaux's top priority, with regard to these deacons and elders, was to get them to function "as one body so as to speak and act as one from the same authority . . . to avoid division."[30] That is why he held quarterly instructional sessions with them as a body. The Elder considered these sessions important, for these officers were in daily contact with local members. Therefore, he made attendance at quarterly sessions mandatory, and said accordingly, "Anyone not present because of sickness must send a report to the effect that he is inactive. . . . Your wife's illness is not a reasonable excuse."

That ruling applied to the entire body of deacons and elders. There was, however, a specific rule regarding attendance for ministers since they were exhorters. "Any minister not meeting quarterly . . . unless because of sickness or death" could not preach. Michaux wanted to be sure they were continuously exposed to his directives and instruction about teaching and preaching from the pulpit.[31]

Elders were not to be at liberty when preaching, not even to follow dictates of the Holy Spirit, because Michaux dictated length and general content of sermons. He limited preachers to forty-five minute sermons, but they could be given a grace period of ten minutes by local deacons in his absence.[32] He also directed them to encourage members in their sermons and never to rebuke. Rebuking was reserved for him and Mrs. Michaux. The Elder explained, "I'm their father in the gospel. Now when you preach, all of your sermons must be based on preaching the humility of Christ, the wonders of the Lord, and the beauty of the Saints."[33] His fear was that local elders might drive members from the churches if they rebuked them. Apparently, reacting to an elder who insisted on rebuking from the pulpit, Michaux implored, "Go out in the field and gather someone together whom you can beat up. . . . Don't beat up mine. I know how to deal with my children."[34]

He was determined to deny elders and deacons an opportunity to challenge his authority as leader, but they sometimes could influence change within the church, though not changes in administration. An example of the kind of change they could influence is as follows. One night, in the mid-1950s, when Michaux no longer had a telecast, a youthful, zealous preacher in the Newport News church got up to deliver his testimony. Few people were in church that night, so in the midst of testifying, he explained why. Members stayed home, he said, to watch television. He opposed saints' watching television, calling it sinful with half-naked women dancing across the screen, with beer and cigarette commercials. Some members, of course, turned television sound down when these annoyances came on. Mrs. Michaux already was in the audience, and the Elder was due any moment. She was moved by what the preacher said and bolted to her feet as soon as he finished the testimony, saying "All saints should get rid of their televisions." When the Elder arrived, he was informed of what had happened and supported his wife on her position. They called for a show of hands of all who would obey. Members did obey. Some sold their televisions, others gave them away, several hid them in attics or turned screens to the wall and covered the set. A few years later everyone had televisions in their homes again. Mrs. Michaux even went out and purchased one, which was sitting in the house in Washington when her husband returned from a trip. He told her to return it to the store because she had spoken against watching television before a congregation and had spread the word to other churches. But she, like other members, had come to believe it was not sinful after all. In retrospect, the Elder televised church services at one time, and recently he had been urging the infirm, elderly, and parents with children to buy televisions for entertainment during lonely hours and to help keep the youth home and off the streets. The influence that the young preacher initially had, though indirectly through Mrs. Michaux, was a rare occurrence for anyone except the Elder and his wife.

More typically Michaux kept elders and deacons in their places of subordination to him. They did not directly influence decisions, and more crucially, he did not name an assistant. Wanting them to make no mistake about their subordinate position, Michaux stated flatly, "No deacon or elder is to consider himself a head official in his local church."[35] The only "head official" any place within that organization was the Elder, the founder. If preachers desired to start their own missions, they were free to do so. Yet, because Michaux made it clear that these missions were to be founded under auspices of the Church of God, preachers with missions were subject to the same rules as those in the already established churches.

For those who might decide to leave the church, Michaux had words of caution:

> Don't pay any attention to the things your imagination tells you you can do—how you can preach, how you can do this or that—about the only thing you can do is to blow your top. . . . Remain one and you will be powerful. . . . I don't care how secure the limbs seem to be on a tree . . . they are no good if the trunk of the tree doesn't hold them up. . . . Cut one of them off and throw it down, then you watch it and see if it doesn't wither and die.[36]

A talented, popular, middle-aged preacher in Washington decided to strike out on his own in 1949, and several members followed him out of the Washington church. He long had been fed up with the paltry sum Michaux gave preachers whom he sent to run revivals in the various churches. He thought, too, that Michaux treated deacons and elders like children, not allowing them to offer opinions, to criticize such rules as "your wife's illness is not a reasonable excuse" for absence from quarterly meetings. But the "straw that broke the camel's back," he said, occurred the day a man came to see Michaux, when this preacher was present with the Elder, and asked if he could talk with him. The Elder said he didn't have time to talk with the brother. "That was a brother who paid his offerings, who had a family, and Elder didn't have time to talk to him. He had time to take his money. Elder was too big to have time to talk to that little man. I decided that was enough and left." Michaux tried to block his leaving. First he tried to take his license to preach, but the man said he still was licensed, with or without the paper as documentation. Next, Michaux tried to sue him for $300 that the man had borrowed from the church. So the preacher engaged a lawyer to defend him but would not file a countersuit for back wages the church "owed" him although the lawyer gleefully urged that action, saying, "We have been trying to get something on Michaux." The preacher stopped short of a countersuit because he remembered something the Elder said, "You can't win fighting!" Today this minister has a prosperous church in Washington, and he has broadcasted every week for thirty years. While the Elder lived, members of the Church of God occasionally would visit that preacher's church just as some still do.[37]

That preacher's was not the only potential ignitable fuse within the camp. Deacons and elders grumbled among themselves about low pay they got when taking leave from their jobs and families to go on special missions for the church, and they complained about not being paid at all for numerous services rendered to the church. A most obvious source of discontent was Michaux's failure to provide a training program for ministers. Many thought their licenses would be worthless outside the Church of God. The preacher who left summed up the conditions of elders and deacons like this: "By not being allowed to raise questions or make comments in meetings, many deacons and elders lost their character, and their authority was inconsequential."

Most members accepted Michaux's brand of leadership, at least tacitly, because they believed affiliation with his church had improved their lives and led them to a new birth. This rebirth issued from a psychological reorganization which permitted them to reject their former life-styles and to accept the standards, practices, and discipline of the Church of God. Indicative of their changed attitudes was the reference to themselves as saints and that also is how Michaux consistently referred to them after 1964. He said mere professing Christians were not recognized by God because they were only so-called Christians and did not adhere strictly to the teachings of Christ. Furthermore, Michaux concluded, the name Christian was used in early Rome to cast aspersion upon followers of Christ. This division of Saints and Christians came late in Michaux's ministry. Until July 4, 1964, he used the term Christian interchangeably with saint. He said it suddenly dawned upon him that he was not always calling members what God would prefer them to be called. He based his new thinking on the numerous references to saints in the Bible.

Members believed they had experienced a rebirth. One elderly member poignantly voiced sentiments of many when she reflected back over her old life:

> As a youth, I had attended church, but people did not preach what even I had in my mind [about how a holy person should live]. I would look up at the sky and ask the Lord to help me. Sometimes after taking a bath, I would ask the Lord to teach me to be clean inside like I was outside.[38]

Another elderly sister testified about her long search for a church which could help improve the quality of her life. She thought her life improved as she stopped playing cards and attending movies. Her mother longed to see those habits disappear and influenced the daughter's search for an "improved" life. She began the search early. Her family migrated from Nansemond County, Virginia, to Newport News. When she was just a child, they periodically traveled back and forth to the eastern shore of Virginia to perform farm labor during the fruit and vegetable picking seasons. That family was Baptist, but at fourteen the girl began attending a Holiness church. The family's pastor was disturbed over the girl's action and urged her mother to persuade the daughter to return to the Baptist fellowship. When she did, under pressure, the preacher asked her why she left, and the girl replied, "because the Holiness church had higher standards and I wanted to be baptized and live right." Her observation that established churches no longer taught sanctification was a common complaint among black folk by the late nineteenth century. The young woman promptly was baptized by the Baptist preacher and remained in that church until 1921, when at the age of eighteen, she joined the Church of God. She recalled in later years how she happened to hear about that church.

> I heard a member talking to my mother about the church and prayer band. I told her that I wished they would come to our house, and she [the mother's friend] arranged for this. When the band came, my mother and older sister sat with them and heard the prayers and lesson and testimony while I passed back and forth through the living room, cleaning the house. When eventually Mrs. Michaux asked them if they wanted to join church, neither my mother or sister wanted to, so she said, "Maybe the girl would like to join." I readily agreed, and she invited me to church so "Brother Michaux" [as she called him] could take me in.[39]

The young woman was baptized again, since Michaux would not accept another church's baptism, and has been in the church over fifty years.

One of the Elder's first 150 members, a migrant from rural North Carolina, told this story about her long, youthful search for a church and gospel which would change her life in a way that established churches had not.

> I heard about Elder Michaux from a woman who lived in Dawson City. She said to me, "Mrs. ———, holy people are on Nineteenth Street preaching, and you should hear them." I told her I wasn't thinking about those tongue people [which I thought they must be]. I had seen plenty [church people singing, preaching, and shouting with] their black robes, on the beach with tamborines, speaking in tongues.

Now, two other Dawson City women and I were already visiting a number of churches, hoping to find the right one. At a Baptist church, they took up collection before preaching, and the preacher said he would not preach before he got $25. He got it. When he started preaching, he said, "Close all the windows; nobody is going to hear who did not pay." And when he preached, you didn't hear nothing. One of the women with us got happy and fell out—women often got happy in church and would run and fall out on some man. This woman fell out, and I said she is not happy; don't hold her. On the way home, she said a bad word.

One of these two women went to hear Elder Michaux. She told me I should "go to see what they were talking and singing about. That first night Sister Michaux was singing "My Savior Now Is Feeding Me with Honey from the Rock." It was so sweet, I joined that very night.[40]

Unfortunately, their saintly interests did not extend often outside the congregation. They were indoctrinated to think of themselves as exclusive and that precluded their interest in offering charity abroad. The church was an inner world outside of which members functioned mainly to earn a salary. The exception was a handful of naturally kind ones who collected for heart or cancer funds and aided all the needy with whom they had contact. According to their neighbors, there were members who would not even permit a stranger to use their porches as shelters from a rain storm.

For many members, conversion had its practical side. They spoke of sin as being an illness which made them moan and groan, which caused mental anguish and physical abuse, which made them feel unclean. After conversion, they claimed psychological solace. They no longer worried, for example, that the policeman on the beat was coming to arrest them since they had committed no crimes. As saints, then, they were happier. Some of them believed, moreover, they were better off economically because they no longer squandered money on liquor, gambling, numbers, women, or jail fines.

There were those who appreciated Michaux's leadership because they learned to balance a budget after joining the church, for they were expected to give offerings as well as meet personal expenses. Many, who rented houses or apartments when they joined the church, later purchased homes and other property, stocks and bonds, and several educated their children and/or grandchildren. These achievements were important measurements of righteousness among members. That is why they testified about these material blessings in church. They wanted everyone to know that God was blessing them because of their righteousness.[41]

Members who joined the church after the 1920s, including the era of the Great Depression, were not basically different in socioeconomic standing from those early ones. Post–1920s joiners were mostly newcomers to Washington, Philadelphia, or New York from the South, with a sprinkling from the West Indies. These migrants sought stability and employment in their new urban settings. Whatever their plight had been, these large cities hardly made it better, and it was probably worse when the depression lingered so long. Established denominations usually did not provide spiritual succor needed by migrants who were caught in the fear and loneliness of social transition and economic depression. Those who joined churches often flocked to storefronts and to exotic temples because they recognized in them qualities of transitional stations, places of comfort. Storefronts and other "nonnormative" religious gatherings provided an intimate and friendly atmosphere for worship and fellowship amidst a new, unfriendly, awesome, urban setting. The Church of God was a transitional station for many, even in its radio ministry. Michaux had tuned his ministry to sound out needs and frustrations of the depressed and to formulate a regimen of treatment for their souls. In addition to black southern-styled revivals and services of gospel preaching, singing, testifying, praying for the healing of wounded souls, Michaux and his staff found jobs for the unemployed and gave food and shelter to the penniless during the depression.

Members who joined after the depression had more varied employment backgrounds in northern cities than in southern ones. Some worked in Civil Service and a few were in the employ of Washington's elite—the Eisenhowers, Congressmen, bankers. In the several cities, men were porters and chauffeurs for banks and department stores, while their wives and single women were domestics, beauticians, seamstresses, and school teachers. A large number of men were self-employed as barbers, photographers, electricians, automobile mechanics, taxi drivers, tailors, carpenters, and junk dealers. One man was an attorney and ex-convict. He became Michaux's private secretary and editor of *Happy News*.[42]

Members offered thanks to God and were loyal to Michaux for pointing them to avenues of gradual material prosperity and contentment. Some believed continued success was dependent upon their loyalty to the collective group, and many vowed "not to bring any reproach on the church" by reverting to sin. One woman testified that she "would live right for meanness." Most members showed dependence on Michaux as one who had rekindled their hope and as one who could empathize with them in their troubles or offer advice and prayer for them during adversity. A *Happy News* article informed the public of members' "childlike dependence." They "come to him with all manner of cares. . . . They seem to think he can do all things. They even come with their headaches, pains and sicknesses. . . . He lays his hands on them, closes his eyes and calls on his heavenly Father to heal these sick hearts." The romanticizing in that article, notwithstanding, more than a few members often showed themselves to be dependent on Michaux and that made it easier for him to control them.[43]

Among those who joined the Church of God large numbers came out of established denominations. If more than one or two previously followed Father Divine or Daddy Grace or were part of assemblies that spoke in tongues, they were reluctant to admit it for fear they would attract Mrs. Michaux's vituperative attacks. She believed religious leaders who boasted of being "divine" were un-Christian and un-Godly. She was especially antipathetic toward former "Grace-ites" and "tongue people," which was her way of referring to those who speak in tongues. Mrs. Michaux believed they were forever spiritually deluded and could not be trusted to live righteously. Her dislike and focus on the "Grace-ites" stemmed from Bishop Grace's dramatic attack on the Church of God in Newport News, where he founded a temple later in the 1920s. He prophesied that the building, which housed Michaux's sanctuary, was going to tumble down and led his congregation in a march around it, threatening to compel the fall. Michaux took Grace's move to be just a stunt and was not admittedly annoyed.[44]

As young people married and began to rear families, the Church of God had a natural population increase from 1919 on. These offspring remained in the church after they became adults, and much intermarriage occurred among them. The size of Michaux's membership remained a guarded secret, however. Many social and religious movements leave such figures unpublished so that the group will seem more influential. Considering his following, though, the composite of visible members of the church and of regular radio listeners and Baptizing attendees, Michaux claimed millions in the 1930s and 1940s. While the actual membership cannot be determined fully, an estimate can be offered: There were 15,000 copies of *Happy News* issued each month from 1936 to 1968. Each member received twelve copies to sell or give away, and pay for, during that period. If these papers were divided equally among the membership, there were 1,250 to get twelve papers each.[45] But many, many papers were left each month without takers. The exact membership was one of Michaux's best kept secrets, second only to his age.

Whatever the numbers Michaux reigned supreme over his members. He told members, in fact, "that he could not be fired because he had not been hired." He claimed a wide range of uncontested powers for himself and was the church's auspicious generalissimo. Leaving nothing to chance, he alone issued administrative, legislative, and adjudicative directives. Clarifying his position of dominance, he said to the deacons and elders seated before him in one assembly, "As your leader, I am trying to set up a constitution for the church to be governed through officers . . . after I am gone."[46] Nobody dared ask: What officers? Or, may I offer suggestions since I teach government, economics? Not a question was raised, not a smirk or quizzical expression crossed a single face. Michaux had just made a sweeping statement about church administration, present and future. The deacons and elders were reminded again, by that statement, that Michaux operated unilaterally; he was the single, governing officer. Any other officer was a rubber stamper. Those present did not seem to realize that he, having no opposition from them, had just wrested authority to write the constitution without their input. If they realized this, they felt powerless to question the Elder. The general responses of members to Michaux's authoritarian control over their lives raises questions about the concept of rebirth with regard to them. Was their conversion more a reconception to a womb-like state of dependence and isolated protection from the realities and adult responsibilities of life than actual rebirth to self-autonomy under God? Were they fully reborn?

Michaux's formative and early adult years occurred at a time in history when people often deferred to strong leaders. He believed this was the way for him to accomplish his goals for the church. In response to domination, he clearly expected deference from members. With his authority entrenched, he set his mind to the business of the church.

7

A Business of Religion

After 1940, second to Michaux's interest in maintaining a loyal, church-centered congregation was his passionate pursuit of a strong financial base for the church. All but a select few viewed his economic manuevers from the sideline. No one, other than himself, was privy to a complete picture of these operations although some members were aware of details of isolated transactions. Mrs. Michaux certainly was least informed. She was not even privy to congregational gossip about financial matters. It was she, however, who captured the attitude of many when she stood erectly before the congregation and tearfully pleaded, "Saints, please pray for Elder that his soul will not be lost. God called him to preach to save souls, not to buy buildings. I'd rather see him dead than so mixed up in business." That was in the 1950s, a time when many members also were concerned that Michaux had shifted ministerial emphasis from spiritual to material matters and had lost balance between the two.

Much of their concern stemmed from the fact that by 1951, Michaux received bad press that raised questions about his business ethics. Sometimes his associates in political circles were implicated along with him. Such was the case when a Senate Banking Subcommittee considered investigating federal lending institutions in 1951 for probable favoritism shown Michaux. At that time a prominent Washingtonian, George Allen, was implicated. That situation originated out of Michaux's tangled designs to develop and expand the black, middle-class, Mayfair Mansions apartment complex in Washington. To best evaluate the merits of these implications one must be aware of allegations surrounding Michaux's acquisition of land upon which the complex stands.

The Elder acted in seeming duplicity even to obtain the land on which he later built the project. The old Benning Race Track had been located on that site when horse racing was legal in the District, from the turn of the century until 1908. After a New York racing promoter named O'Hara purchased the track, return of the sport seemed certain. A bill to relegalize the sport in the District was introduced in Congress. In March of 1940, it was pending. The Senate District Commission already had held hearings on that proposal. Passage seemed certain because the bill had widespread backing although newpapers joined with other forces to keep horse racing banned. One crucial supporter was George Allen, a commissioner of the District. He owned a race horse and was scheduled to testify before the Senate committee in favor of the bill's passage. Allen also was an honorary deacon in Michaux's Radio Church of God. When Michaux, who opposed horse racing, heard of Allen's intention, he dispatched the following telegram to Allen.

It has been brought to the attention of the membership of the [Radio] Church of God at Washington of which you are an honorary deacon that you own a race horse and that you are to appear today for the Senate Committee hearings on the passage of the bill introduced by Senator Reynolds which, if passed, will permit racing and betting on races in the District of Columbia. Though some may not consider betting on horses a vice, it is considered so by all religious bodies and orthodox churches. Therefore, knowing your respect for all such

bodies, you are requested to register your objections to the passage
of this bill and also to offer your race horses for sale at this hearing to
Senator Reynolds or William C. Murphy or any of the supporters of
this bill at 50% of what the horses [sic] cost you. Done by order of
the Church now covening at Philadelphia. Please read this telegram
at the hearing, answer if possible and also publish the same in all
local papers so they know our stand and yours.[1]

If any other association than that of honorary affiliate with the
church existed between Michaux and Allen at that time, it is unknown.
Thus, on the face of it, this telegram is audacious. Interestingly
enough, Allen did not support the bill in his testimony, and he
offered his horse for sale to Senator Reynolds.[2] Without Allen's
support the bill was defeated. A few months later Mayfair Mansions,
Inc., in which Michaux's leadership was prominent, purchased the
race track for the housing project. Allen was a shareholder, having
one of the five shares of stock in the project.[3]

Construction began during the winter of 1942. At that time the
general contractor was personally assured by the National Housing
Agency that the project was an administration job and that all
funds necessary for its completion would be provided by appropriate
government agencies. That next year Michaux informed the Commissioner of the Federal Housing Agency and the administrator of
the NHA that the initial mortgage of $2,478,000 was insufficient, and
he requested additional financing. Commissioner Abner W. Ferguson
(FHA) denied the request, stating that the World War II emergency
precluded further financial assistance to such projects. Michaux
successfully contended for the funds, but when he finally received
them, job costs had escalated, surpassing previous estimated costs.
Instead of just $337,000, $682,578 was needed for completion of the
housing. FHA officials referred Michaux to the Reconstruction Finance
Corporation for excess funding above $337,000, but Ferguson tried
to dissuade RFC from granting additional funds. To scale this hurdle
Michaux asked people close to the president for help.[4]

He wrote to Mrs. Mary Bethune, the former Director of Negro
Affairs in the National Youth Administration, whom he claimed as
a friend, about the matter. "Our dealings," he stated,

with the RFC Mortgage Company to get this additional sum of $345,000
were progressing satisfactorily until Commissioner Ferguson injected
the view that foreclosure of the project would be the best way out. . . .
We [directors of Mayfair Mansions] feel that through Mr. Ferguson's
attitude, the door of RFC Mortgage Company has been shut in our
faces. . . . We have only until February 2, 1944, [to get the $345,000] . . .
because Mr. Ferguson plans foreclosure at [that] time.[5]

That was less than one week from the date of the letter to Mrs.
Bethune, and Michaux asked her to solicit help from their "mutual
friend, Mrs. Roosevelt." He wrote yet another letter to Steven Early,
secretary to the president and an honorary junior deacon in the
Radio Church of God, about the matter.[6]

Michaux promoted his cause as racial. In writing to Mrs. Bethune,
he explained that the building of Mayfair Mansions was the "first
and only opportunity Negroes had in any administration to establish
and prove their ability to build, and occupy and pay for a project
costing $3,160,000 and insured by the Federal Government. . . .
Should [this] project be foreclosed, [it] would ruin the chances of
the Negro Race ever having such an opportunity again for at least
a generation."[7] He charged Ferguson with having ill will toward
Negroes since the commissioner had said "on many occasions the
housing project was too good for Negroes." The letter continued,
"In this case I feel that his object is solely to deprive Negro leadership of the accomplishment of successfully executing such a project
and give it back to Negroes at a greatly increased cost to the government . . . just to prove that Negro leadership is a failure in large
matters."[8]

Responding to the urgency of the matter, Mrs. Bethune forwarded
the Elder's letter to the First Lady and asked her to intercede. Eleanor
Roosevelt contacted proper officials who held a meeting with Mayfair Mansions directors. After denying charges of racism, FHA
officials countered Michaux's charges concerning their motives by
pointing out how the agency had insured numerous housing projects
occupied by—but not constructed by—Negroes. To make good their
defense, they again referred Michaux to RFC. This time, however, he
received necessary funding to complete the project despite the fact that

such leading white liberal New Dealers as Will W. Alexander, a co-director for Race Relations at the Julius Rosenwald Fund, protested to Mrs. Roosevelt that the housing development was being financially mismanaged.[9]

Michaux seemed to mismanage business. Throughout the years he continuously applied for loans to expand Mayfair Mansions and to extricate the project from financial difficulties. While this kind of manuevering often is routine in business, what confused the issue was Michaux's success in obtaining loans for developing Mayfair Mansions from RFC despite his delinquency in making payments. Michaux was black, and black folk were not expected by other blacks nor whites to succussfully maneuver business deals at this level over and over. That was the concern of the Banking Subcommittee in 1951.[10] The committee suspected favoritism was shown Michaux because George Allen became a director of RFC during the Truman administration and the Elder's most recent loan had been granted through that agency in 1949.[11]

Allen, who had sold his shares in Mayfair Mansions, was not available for comment on the matter when it hit the press. But one of Michaux's associates, the former Washington, D.C., Judge James Cobb, told reporters, "Mr. Allen and Michaux were very close, and Mr. Allen helped manipulate these loans."[12] Stopping short of accusing President Truman of intervening in RFC matters in Michaux's behalf Cobb claimed "he had once accompanied Michaux to the White House to see President Truman." This judge had attended the Elder's services frequently and was an occasional dinner guest in his home, and his allegations gave the issue basis for validity. Judge Cobb had been one of Michaux's constant companions as had Major Wright.[13] Michaux issued a refutation, claiming "he was 'sure' . . . Allen never helped obtain any RFC loans for the housing development."[14] Apparently the matter ended there so far as the Senate Subcommittee was concerned, for there are no records of an investigation into the loans. Michaux's credibility in financial matters, nevertheless, had been questioned once again in the press. After that commotion, his difficulties with various financial agencies and departments increased.[15]

On September 8, 1953, foreclosure on Mayfair Mansions was authorized by RFC, and maturity on the 1949 loan was accelerated because payments were in arrears. To make matters worse, no taxes were paid on the property from 1948 to 1951.[16] Foreclosure was not completed, though, and early in 1960 the Treasury Department still was trying to collect delinquent taxes and to foreclose the 1949 loan which had matured in June of 1959. Curiously, but for unknown reasons, officials in the Treasury Department sent memos to the White House about the Elder's difficulties. These were informative about the Elder's financial crisis without either offering or overtly requesting suggestions for resolving it.[17] Michaux was undaunted, if he knew about the memos, and late in 1960, he made plans to build another housing project on marsh land adjacent to Mayfair Mansions. The Redevelopment Land Agency challenged the proposal, announcing that no Michaux project would be approved until his fiscal problems with the Treasury Department were resolved. This housing was to be an urban renewal project and required RLA support to qualify for federal mortgage insurance.[18] Michaux's lawyer, Arthur Chaite, promised that the Elder would settle all delinquent accounts when RLA approved the project.[19] Details of how Michaux arranged his business to qualify for RLA approval of the new housing are hazy, but he did make legal corporate changes in the church's structural organization.

On March 13, 1964, he changed the name of the religious operation from Church of God and the Gospel Spreading Association to Gospel Spreading Church, Inc.[20] This action has been interpreted by corporation lawyers as making members legal owners of church holdings and the church's business enterprises nontaxable. Yet, there are indications that certain pieces of property, such as Mayfair Mansions, may have been placed in Michaux's name and in names of staff in Washington so he could be free to utilize them to the church's financial benefit without jeopardizing all of the property. Mayfair Mansions, Inc., for example, was not transferred to the Gospel Spreading Church, Inc. until February 1, 1972, more than four years after the Elder's death. By 1966 Michaux had complied with federal requisites on taxes and loans, for he received 6 million dollars in FHA loans to build Paradise Manor, a 617 apartment complex on twenty acres adjacent to Mayfair Mansions, which was completed after his death in 1968.[21]

In spite of financial entanglements, Michaux managed to stall foreclosures and to avoid prosecution for nonpayment of back taxes. No doubt he convinced authorities that he was innocent of criminal intent by conjuring up the image of an inscrutable man-of-the-cloth. He sometimes tried to extricate himself from difficulties with federal authorities with comments like, "I'm a preacher who knows nothing about business. What am I doing over here in the business world anyway? Let me get back over to preaching where I know what I am doing." He had adequate skills for small business dealings, but they alone were not applicable to this more complex business situation. Therefore, Michaux devised other means of dealing successfully. He often took business friends and legal experts along as spokesmen. On those occasions, the Elder "dealt himself out" of discussions while his spokesmen drove hard bargains at his command. He dramatized, feigned withdrawal during such sessions by sitting with eyes closed, claiming a mood of pensiveness, meditation or mysticism. Sometimes those on the other side of negotiating observed that Michaux was asleep; as if he had not been carefully attentive all the while, he pretended to be aroused when nudged. He believed those with whom he negotiated detected a possibility of innocence, or ineptness, as well as a desire to resolve the crisis at hand, from his mood. Though Michaux often was on the brink of foreclosure or prosecution or investigation, those who could have pressed him to the fullness of the law retreated or gave enough slack to permit Michaux to save face and property.[22]

Beneath the calm facade was anxious concern. Perceptive members discerned this when Michaux made queries of them such as: "How many of you would be willing to give up everything you own for the good of the church?" Many thought the question was rhetorical, raised to test loyalty. The few with insight into the church's financial crises, like the field representative, understood the cryptic message. They shuddered at the prospect of the actual losses members would incur if Michaux asked them to make this ultimate sacrifice to save property from foreclosure or seizure by the Internal Revenue Service and funding agencies.[23]

If he had little ability for business management, the Elder proved himself to have considerable knack for finding capital and valuable property. Referring to this, one reporter explained that he should "not be passed off as just another gospel spreader . . . but should be regarded as a shrewd businessman," who at the time of his death had chiseled out an estate valued at more than twenty million dollars.[24] This estate consisted of temples for worship, apartments, housing developments in Washington and in Newport News, 1,800 acres of land in Jamestown, the National Memorial land, 636 acres in Charles City County, Virginia, and scattered buildings, houses, and lots from North Carolina to New York and Ohio. No one knows to this day exactly how much property was involved because the Elder registered several pieces in others' names, and some persons may not have surrendered that which they held after his death.[25]

For Michaux each purchase was a major business deal to be evaluated in terms of immediate profit and future worth. He evinced this attitude when he boasted on one occasion, "We have property all over, and I have been wise enough to get . . . [it] on commercial thoroughfares, so that no matter what comes the property will increase in value rather than decrease."[26] He often recalled that in the beginning, before he seceded from the Church of Christ (Holiness), the church had been poor. A patched-up tent served as the place of worship, during coldness of winter weather, until enough money was saved from offerings to rent a small house. Even before he was independent, Michaux set up the Gospel Spreading Tabernacle Building Association. It was incorporated under Virginia laws on February 26, 1921, to receive funds, pay debts, and purchase property for the church.[27] The GSTBA's immediate purpose was to accumulate funds. During that early period, when Michaux was in his own church, neither he nor other church officials received salaries. As pastor, he accepted a monthly free-will offering, and Elder Howard W. Poole, secretary-treasurer, got free room and board in the Building. Other officers, including elders, supported themselves and their families by working full-time outside the church.[28]

To fill its coffers the GSTBA relied mainly on traditional sources, such as offerings and tithing. Between 1921 and 1925, Michaux instituted a series of weekly offerings: Half-Day or tithing, Building Fund (twenty-five cents), Sacrificial Offering (a week's income every four months), and occasional vouchers. After the depression, he set up burial and travel funds into which each participating member paid twenty-five and fifty cents per week, respectively. These latter two funds entitled them to a church-financed burial and to two annual round-trips to one of the churches in another city on special occasions.[29]

Near the end of each service members went, in procession, to place tithes, offerings, and other funds on a table in front of the pulpit. Two deacons accepted and counted monies before the congregation while a church secretary recorded names of contributors and amounts they gave. Each local church's expenses were paid from these monies, and the remainder was sent to Washington where Michaux located business headquarters in 1929.[30]

In addition to money, members contributed labor and talent to help the church advance. A group of women, for example, formed a circle in the late 1930s called Willing Workers. They made articles of clothing, bed and table linens, cooked dinners, baked bread and pastries, and sold these products so they could place money in the church's treasury.[31] Whenever necessary, men donated labor to build and repair church property. Although Michaux expected all members to make a contribution of some kind, no one neglecting to do so was dismissed from the church for that cause.[32]

There were members and nonmembers alike who accused Michaux of being greedy for money as they observed the system of giving he established. Yet, his system hardly was different from established black church collections. A perennial accusation against black preachers, moreover, is that they all are greedy for money. Generally they request offerings, tithes, special gifts for rallies and other drives. What made Michaux's system appear unusual was the visibility of his compulsion to accumulate property and other capital in addition to church edifices. He embarked upon this venture at a time when established churches, black and white, often were content just to own an edifice for worship and fellowship and to keep operating expenses current. Funds like sacrificial offering sounded horrid to a poor people although they generally gave as much to their churches annually as Michaux's members gave to the Church of God. Add vouchers to the horrid sounding sacrificial offerings. The Elder asked for vouchers to bail the church out of financial difficulties as well as to help provide seed money for real estate investments and evangelism.

The Church of God saw many difficult days, for valuable property was almost lost several times because mortgage payments were delinquent and taxes had not been paid.[33] The old GSTBA, for example, had contracted terms for purchasing the Lincoln theater as a place for worship prior to 1929. Suffering from overextension as the church expanded, the GSTBA was in a moribund state. In an effort to bail out, Michaux reorganized the business organ in 1929 and named it the Gospel Spreading Association. New deeds were written and financing terms were readjusted for the new GSA, and delinquent mortgages on church property were not foreclosed.[34] Less than a decade later the superintendent of the National Historic Park at Yorktown, Floyd Flickinger, said he was "informed from very reliable sources that . . . there would probably be a foreclosure on the property Michaux was acquiring" in Jamestown.[35] Flickinger's information was accurate. Michaux fervently petitioned his banker friends, the Wrights of Philadelphia, to negotiate a loan for $10,000 to pay on the Jamestown tract in 1937, shortly after his National Memorial fund-raising drive collapsed.[36]

If financial pressures and ambitions were not incentive enough to motivate members to give freely to the church, Michaux tried to convince them that there were personal benefits to be gained from giving. He told anecdotes about how God had blessed those who gave freely to encourage others to tithe and give offerings. One of his favorite stories was one about Rudolph Jones, then a successful scrap iron and metal dealer in Hampton. Jones shared it with the congregation and Michaux years before, and he listened as the Elder repeated the story to other deacons and to the elders assembled.

> I wish I had time to let Brother Rudolph Jones tell his story pertaining to his first sacrificial [offering]. I'll tell you as much as I can remember. When he came into the Church he had a wife who is a godly woman. . . . When Brother Rudolph first faced a test concerning his sacrificial offerings, he didn't have money enough to pay his rent. He only had $11.00. His wife told him that sacrificial was due and for him to pay that and let everything else go until they got some more money. . . . He told her all right but insinuated that they would have to go out in the street. . . . Nevertheless he brought it in. He was just starting in the junk business and he had an old truck.
>
> After he had given his sacrificial, the spirit of the Lord came upon him and gave him foolish boldness. . . . Brother Rudolph went down to the place where they were selling brand new trucks. There he told the man he wanted to get a truck. The man talked with him, telling

him the price required for a down payment, told him all about the truck just as though Brother Rudolph was ready to close the deal. After the man got everything lined up Brother Jones told him . . . he didn't have any money. The man said . . . You mean to say you're trying to buy a brand new truck and don't have any money. Why you must be crazy. . . . The man somewhat admired him . . . [and looked on] as Brother Jones and the big boss were talking. Then the manager turned to the salesman and said . . . I'm going to let him have that truck. Go on and write it up for him. . . . When Brother Rudolph got ready to go, he told the man he didn't have any gas. The man said why don't you have enough money to pay for gas? . . . Go and let him have some gas too. Let's see what is in him. . . . When he got ready to pull off he didn't have tags. Lo and behold the man even went ahead and paid for the tags and Brother Jones left there with a brand new truck. . . . Not a cent! But he had paid his sacrificial.[37]

Michaux's reason for repeating this story was obvious. He hoped those who heard would deduce from it that because Jones paid sacrificial offering the Lord gave him courage to ask for a truck, and the Lord moved on the dealer's heart to let him have the truck. Then Jones used the truck to begin building a million dollar business. Indeed, other members tried this approach and because of their audacity and reasonably good credit rating dealers sold them houses and automobiles without or with very small down payments.

One could expect to have not only individual material possessions increased after giving offerings but to be healed of illnesses, according to Michaux. To document this idea, he repeated the story told by an elderly sister in the Washington church.

"The Lord told me that if I paid my sacrificial, He was going to bless me, . . . And I paid . . . [it] last Friday. . . . " She said that she had been wearing glasses because she could not hardly see very good. So while lying down in the bed . . . by herself, she said the Lord told her to pick up her Bible, which was laying over on the other pillow, and read the 91st Psalm. She picked up the Bible and read that. Then He told her to read the Fiftieth Psalm, where it says, pay thy vows, call upon me and I will deliver you if you get in trouble. And still . . . another passage. Then all at once she realized that she was reading without her glasses. [In her testimony, she said,] "Look here; I don't have my glasses on; for I could hardly see even with them on, but today I can see even better than ever before!" She said she jumped out of the bed and began to shout and praise the Lord all around the room. She said she got to the place where she felt that she could run through troops and leap over the walls. And while she was feeling that way, the devil said jump out of the window.[38]

Michaux had made his point.

Black churches have served their congregations in multi-institutional ways. An important service historically was that of social work. Around the turn of the century, black trained clergy began to concern itself with inspiring social work rather than doing it. After the Great Depression, even members in the Church of God did not think they received enough help from the church. It may be that Michaux had to try to motivate them to give because no direct benefits accrued to them through the church. Therefore, Michaux's pep talks about how necessary offerings and tithes were to help members in financial crises too often fell on deaf ears. Experience taught most members to be less impressed with Michaux's motivational talks than with his attached rider: Members could expect, he said, only to receive financial assistance from the church commensurate to their contributions to it. "When anybody applies or claim they need, we go to the record. . . . I ask what is his record. If he has sung and prayed and did nothing else, I'll say let's go around and sing and pray with him."[39]

Members believed him. Some of them had given freely and consistently, but Michaux told them he couldn't help them when they needed assistance. There were instances in which those who had savings accounts with the church were told, by clerks in the office, that they could not withdraw savings at that time and would have to wait. Michaux would ask elderly ones, who came seeking assistance, "Have you tried welfare?" "Do you have relatives?" "Can they help you?" These were heart-rending questions, after teaching them to rely on the church for assistance rather than on the state and following instructions that members should forsake relationships outside the membership.

Certain funds did not function to members' satisfaction. The Burial Fund, for instance, was not used to provide for the deceased in a manner that generally pleased members. After paying into that fund, sometimes for twenty years or more, one received a pauper's burial. Even the man who had been secretary of the church for more than a quarter century, receiving marginal income, had a cheap burial. To members' dismay he was laid out in a black pine box. That was in the "progressive" and "protesting" decade of the 1960s. Several members became disgusted enough to swamp the Elder with protests, forcing him to order a better coffin for the deceased one who had served the church faithfully. This and similar examples taught many members the wisdom of providing for personal family needs before giving to the church because where Michaux's financial program was not lacking, it was abstract.

Evidence of this abstraction was seen in the Elder's exhortation that members should give offerings to enhance the image of the church. He reminded them that collectively people, like God, are known by their works. "The glory of God is the work of God. He is glorified by His works. What you do makes you what you are," he explained. In another motivational pitch, he told them they were making an investment for later economic security and that the "entire wealth of the church [was theirs] as . . . individuals or collectively."[40]

Actually Michaux's intention was to forge his church into a model for black churches. He intended to create a base of economic as well as spiritual power for the Church of God. He urged members, therefore, to work as a unit to inspire others to strive for black economic solidarity. Trying to interpret his vision and ambition to them, he once asked, "Do you see all the skyscrapers, street cars and airplane lines owned by white people? Want to know why they have them? Because they work together. . . . They are not owned by one man but by a group of people who came together as one and pooled their knowledge, finances and built."[41] He pointed out to the assembly that black people already had economic power, that what they needed to do was unite the power and channel it into a positive force for the benefit of the black community. "Today," he said, "our earning power is fifteen billion dollars. . . . All we need to learn is how to get together and use our money. . . . Every other nationality comes with a shovel piling up our money."[42] Michaux's references to the black community's economic power potential and his interests in real estate development moved one contemporary reporter to call him the "practical watchman who works vigorously to improve the lot of the black man."[43] A more accurate observation would have been that Michaux's real interest was in developing an economic empire under his direct leadership. Allusions to interest in advancing the lot of black folk generally were merely incidental to his intention to inspire his congregation to support freely his economic fancies.

Some members believed the Elder's avowed concern over their problems as workers evolved from selfish rather than altruistic motives. Several, who worked in the Newport News Shipyard, were annoyed that he participated in anti-CIO demonstrations in 1944. They reasoned that they would get higher salaries and better benefits through the CIO, but Michaux was afraid a big union would create periods of unemployment through strikes. So he joined the rallies to help keep the CIO out in favor of the company union, the Peninsula Shipbuilders' Association (PSA). He took his Cross Choir to perform on the last night of pro-PSA rallies. In a broadcasted message, he said the CIO was undesirable for two reasons: It creates "industrial strikes" and levies "assessments to replenish the treasury against workers." Although major civic, business, professional, and fraternal organizations backed the CIO, when workers filed to the polls and voted, the PSA won by a three to one margin.[44] Michaux desired a steady inflow of offerings, and, from that perspective, thought a steady income more practical than a high salary interrupted with periods of strikes without pay. He believed that was more practical for the Peninsula's economy. It was more practical for his church's treasury, and he helped persuade workers that it was more practical for them.

Because they believed Michaux was insensitive to their personal financial needs, many members did not contribute freely to the church, and they did not give regularly. Instead they were guided by this policy: Give whatever you can afford to give after expenses and savings whenever you can afford to give. According to Michaux and local officers, the church often was in financial distress because everyone did not contribute a "fair share."[45] In 1956, the Elder bemoaned the fact that half of his members did not tithe or give offerings regularly.[46]

Michaux's insensitivity was not the only factor influencing members' hesitation to give freely, but it probably contributed to an element of suspicion. Michaux refused to make financial reports, and suspicion mounted within the congregation. There was only one financial disclosure during the church's forty-seven year history under the Elder. In the wake of the court suit against him, alleging mishandling of the fund-raising drive in 1937 for the National Memorial project, Michaux gave curious reporters an accounting in 1938. They ran an assessment of the church's property valuation in Washington's *Evening Star*.[47] Thereafter, all financial records were sealed. Several members, who left the church after World War II, complained of this situation.[48] Giving only "lip service" to the pressure, Michaux facetiously alerted officers to be careful with financial records so they could be opened to public examination. He answered reporters' queries about money, though. Leaving the matter there, he never produced records nor made reference to anyone in the organization who would.[49]

This veil of secrecy, together with his lifestyle, caused people outside the church to accuse him of fattening his pockets by duping members into giving money to build a church empire. He was questioned about private possessions. A banker once said to him mockingly, for example, "Elder, that is a mighty good car you drive. What is behind it all; is it psychology? If your Lord were here, do you think He would ride in as good a car as that? Like a flash the Elder replied [in kind], 'No, He would not ride in that car; He would ride in a chariot through the air.' "[50] His being chauffered about the East Coast in Cadillac limousines attracted comments throughout the years. The Elder's lifesyle, however, partially dictated the kinds and numbers of automobiles he owned. He visited each of his five large churches in Newport News, Washington, Baltimore, Philadelphia and New York every week, and he hired a chauffeur and bought comfortable automobiles to make travel more pleasurable. The Michauxs normally kept two cars at their disposal. It rarely was convenient for the Elder to go directly to church from home, and often he attended to business or held rehearsals and meetings following church services. The second car was Mrs. Michaux's so she would not be inconvenienced while he was on business.[51]

They owned houses in Newport News and Washington and kept apartments in church buildings in both cities and in Philadelphia. If they stayed overnight where they had no residence, the Michauxs boarded with a particular family in the church, as was the case frequently in New York.

The couple lived in comfortable residences, neither lavishly nor opulently furnished. The Washington residence, a row house at 1712 R Street NW, and the home on Pinkey's Beach in Newport News were handsomely furnished with grand piano, crystal, silver, gold, and china curios. They were spacious with several bedrooms and bathrooms to accommodate the Michauxs and their guests and relatives. During the 1960s, an elevator-lift was installed in the Washington home for the elderly founders' comfort, but especially for Mrs. Michaux. A chauffeur-valet and cook-maid were responsible for upkeep of these dwellings. Women from local congregations volunteered to clean and cook whenever the Michauxs visited in their cities.[52]

The Elder was aware of grumblings within the church. He told elders and deacons there were members who did not want to give an offering for his support each month because they said he didn't need it. Michaux was so provoked on one occasion that he declared he did not want "a $1,000 to hide away." He said he wanted it to invest for the church's benefit. He sometimes defended himself against accusations of financial mismanagement while accusing others of the same. Once he pleaded, "I neither see nor handle sacrificial. I am not Father Divine nor Bishop Grace."[53] Michaux was perplexed that members did not understand how much money it took to finance revivals, baptizings, building of new church edifices, remodeling, recurring church expenses, and sideliner business, such as markets and cafés. Still that did not include living expenses for him and his wife nor overhead and salaries for those employed by the church.

But members could not understand since they could not see what was happening with money, and business details were neither shared with nor explained to them. Those who gave regularly did so either because they had faith in the Elder or because they believed it was part of their spiritual obligation to contribute to the church, or because they thought blessings would follow in proportion to their gifts, or because of some combination of reasons. Everyone groped in the dark, including Michaux, for he had no comprehensive economic plan. He only had vague glimpses of what he wanted to accomplish. As aspects of the vision unfolded, he relentlessly pursued them until they either became realities or drifted out of reach.

The fact that Michaux had no comprehensive economic blueprint may, in part, explain why Robert Weaver, first secretary of the Department of Housing and Urban Development, made the following observation about him. "During the New Deal period, I came to know Elder Michaux and was able to observe his political and economic activities. There is no doubt in my mind that through personal contacts and his public exposure, he exerted significant political influence. I do not believe his economic theories were generally sound and I have specific differences with his proposals in this field."[54] Unfortunately Mr. Weaver would not identify those "specific differences." But he, like the rest of Michaux's public, recognized that the Elder was trying to build an economic empire. No one understood why, except Michaux, if he did.

A well-developed business plan could have raised and answered pertinent questions to the satisfaction of many, especially of members, such as: To what ends are we, the church, making real estate investments? When will we have invested enough? How will returns be used to benefit members and their posterity? What will become of the estate after the Elder's death? What property belongs to the church? What property belongs to Michaux and his family? Young articulate members raised these questions among themselves and sometimes to their parents. But the answers were locked inside their leader.

Even when he discussed his trying to arrange for the church's future after his death, Michaux was vague. This statement is typical of what he shared on that matter:

Now precious ones, we are getting things straightened out so if at any time, I should pass they will remain in order, for I am experienced and well-versed in business, . . . *another* may not be able to manage things as well as I. We are selecting a trust company to take care of a trust fund and our properties, in order that nobody may come in as a stranger, get among you and divide you and separate your properties. We have fixed it for all of your properties, all of our resources. We are trying to build them up so that our children, our children's children will come along with the spirit and be secure.

. . . In our next meeting we will go through it in detail so that you will understand it and know as a body what you have, what you own and what the value of them are in order that nobody can come along and give you any misleadings.[55]

He articulated such questions as: What belongs to the church? What is the value of the church's property? And he raised additional questions that disturbed members: What "we" were selecting a trust company? What did he mean by "We have fixed it for all of your properties, all of our resources. We are trying to build them up"? None of these questions was answered to members' satisfaction during Michaux's lifetime. Unfortunately, the detailed explanation never came.

In 1966, two years prior to his death, Michaux drew up a constitution and bylaws. That document merged everything under one corporation, changing the Church of God and the Gospel Spreading Association to the Gospel Spreading Church, Inc. Provisions called for a seven member board of directors to direct, control, and manage the corporation. A president would head the board, sign checks, deeds, and other important papers and manage affairs of the corporation. A secretary would keep records, and a bonded treasurer would receive and deposit all corporation funds. No board member could receive monies from the corporation's assets or dividends. They could be reimbursed for expenses accumulated while on business for the church.[56]

Then, the ailing and feeble Elder, in a vaguely worded will dated July 1968, appointed a white man of questionable character to be executor of his black congregation's estate. This mysterious will was preceded by two earlier ones that were drawn up in 1958 and 1966, the year that the church was incorporated as Gospel Spreading Church, Inc. In the 1958 will he bequeathed personal property to his wife, to his brothers and sisters, to his secretary and chauffeur, and appointed his brother, Louis Michaux, and the National Bank of

Washington executors and trustees of his personal estate. In 1966, he appointed his wife executor of his personal estate and dropped his brother from the will. Louis had broken openly from Michaux to support Malcolm X, who by 1966 had been assassinated. The Elder willed Louis' share to Louis' first wife. Because Mrs. Michaux had died in 1967, the Court deferred to the 1958 will and appointed Louis executor of Michaux's personal estate, which was listed at about $250,000.[57] But the judge declared the 1958 will temporarily suspended after the 1968 will was disclosed.

That mysterious will was filed by Michaux in New York City during the summer of 1968 but was not brought to court to be probated until January 1970. To the dismay of the church and Michaux's family it bequeathed all of the Elder's worldly possessions to the congregation of the Gospel Spreading Church and appointed the self-styled, Jewish Reformed "Rabbi" Abraham Abraham the estate's executor. Members thought the rationale Michaux gave in the will for naming the Rabbi executor was questionable. That part read:

> My deacons and elders of the Church know why I selected Rabbi Abraham Abraham, so that peace may reign within the church. His assistance and aid in bringing about serenity and peace in and among the church members, because of no material gain by anyone, will satisfy all the church members.
>
> So long as he shall live, he shall administer these church funds, and I trust that he will select a successor prior to his demise. He is a man of God, and I know he will not fail me or my congregation, because he will be serving God.[58]

Many members resented the Rabbi and several had made Michaux aware of their feelings. They accused the Rabbi of claiming to telephone Michaux from Israel so Michaux could preach over a radio hook-up, when he actually was spotted in a telephone booth in Washington during the time of the alleged telephone conversation "from Israel." Those members said he was a liar and a fortune hunter. Members could not conceive of how his administering of church funds could bring about peace and serenity among them when they resented the Rabbi so much.[59] That part of the will was so incredulous the church group concluded that Michaux had been forced, somehow, into writing it. They were greatly relieved when Judge Charles Richey, U.S. District Court, Washington, D.C., ruled that will invalid and lifted suspension on the one of 1958.[60] With that decision, the Rabbi disappeared from the church scene completely.

The estate has not been settled because the church and family cannot agree on which properties or parts of properties were personally Michaux's or what part of that personal property which the church claims belongs to the family. Neither side will yield to the other, and the problem is deeply rooted. It goes back to the church's beginning. When the Elder's father died in 1921, he took proceeds from his estate and used them as seed money to establish the Church of God and Gospel Spreading Tabernacle Building Association, after leaving the Church of Christ (Holiness) U.S.A. The family claims that money, the amount of which has not been established, and increase from the investment.[61]

Michaux's life, as church leader, had come full-cycle. He began and ended his ministry in the Church of God concentrating on matters of business. In the beginning, he created a structure within which to build an economic empire. In the end, he willed the confusion that virtually dismantled the church's holdings. For almost two months before dying, he lay critically ill but quietly at rest in Freedman's Hospital in Washington. He received few visitors, his sisters, brothers, church officials, and occasionally other members. Those who went to his bedside reported few details about his illness, except to admit it was grave and that the Elder seemingly had no will to live. They reminded members that when Mrs. Michaux died on October 28, 1967, he said he no longer desired to live, and his health immediately deteriorated as often is the habit of elderly bereaved mates. That next year, on Sunday, October 20, 1968, Elder Michaux died. Members were grieved, and they mourned the loss. The Churches of God were draped in mourning cloths, and the founder's body was taken to Newport News for funeral rites and burial after lying in state in the Washington edifice.[62]

Immediately after the funeral and interment, board members, deacons, and elders mobilized, calling meetings, caucusing to decide how to divide the spoils of leadership, how to control the church's wealth.[63]

8

Of Cults and Other Considerations

A study of Michaux's life such as a historical analysis presents invariably annoys an occasional reader because it offers no pat conclusions. Rather it steers the reader away from typecasting and sociological labeling that often present uncomplex, stereotyped conclusions on the whole matter of a complex life. Consequently the reader should not easily fall prey to the vice of categorizing a complex life without pondering over the validity of the appointed labels, and in so doing should call into question the relationship of that life to his/her own. In the past, few who attend established churches have been challenged to question the relationship of Elder Michaux and his members to themselves, either as pastors or bishops or as members. This is because in the American press, Michaux has been handily labeled a cultist, a term which suggests that his behavior and philosophy were categorized as pathological or counter established church. Previous commentaries on the Elder present a terminal case rather than seminal study that sheds enlightenment on the Christian church in the United States. The term cultist has been an obstruction, preventing the study of Michaux as a primary key toward understanding the historical development of the twentieth century church in this country. To broaden the term and to suggest a new basis for discussion of the religious typology— cult—I raise the inevitable question and explore answers to it: Was Michaux a cultist?

The Elder eschewed the label and protested to Miles Mark Fisher, who had so categorized him on pages of *Crisis*, that he was not a cultist.[1] The word cult did then, as it does now, carry a pejorative connotation. Popular opinion holds that cults are bizarre, and members within them are brainwashed, indoctrinated, and manipulated. Many think cults are alien from the dominant culture and a threat to the American social order. The term appears frequently in today's media and was most noticeably headlined in connection with the 1978 Jonestown tragedy in Guyana. Current interest in cults extends beyond that catastrophe, however. There are approximately 3,000 active, fringe religious groups, that some call cults and describe as being of a nonnormative religious strain, in the United States.[2] But years before cults had widespread appeal for young Americans in middle and upper class white society and were then mainly fixtures in ancient and "foreign" literature, observers, of the 1920s and 1930s, wrote that cult-like activities were flourishing in black communities. Writers suggested that the cult was an aberrant form within the black American religious experience. Michaux was insulted that Fisher and some other contemporaries referred to his church as being of this genre. He contended that the Church of God was a remnant of the early Christian church. It was more akin to that early church, he maintained, than were conventional ones in application of Christian principles to daily living. Several charismatic leaders of religious assemblies organized during that period were called cultists by contemporaries. Besides Michaux, Father Divine and Bishop (Daddy) Grace, W. D. Fard and Elijah Muhammad, Mother Rosa Horne, Bishop Ida Robinson, Noble Drew Ali, and F. S. Cherry numbered in that group.[3]

Michaux tried to disassociate himself from such categorizing because he thought it was dangerous, that it threatened to destroy him and his church. He especially was concerned that his church-

business combination was vulnerable, and he nurtured it protect-
ingly against the awesome demise which had befallen Garvey's
United Negro Improvement Association. The UNIA was ill-omened
because Garvey successfully combined within it politics, business,
and religion and flaunted his concoction and following through the
streets of America. It had to be destroyed. With its massive following
and emphasis on virtues of black skin complexion among African
descendants, the UNIA threatened traditional institutional life and
leadership in both white and black America. The relationship between Garvey and new religious leaders called cults is discernible to
the astutely curious. Garvey and the "cultists" attacked organized
Christianity and the established black church, flagrantly merged
the secular with the religious, appealed to masses during an era of
social unrest and attacked white racism. If Michaux did not acknowledge the relationship, he was sensitive to how others categorized
him and moved to protect himself by disassociating from popular
black folk movements, for he remembered lessons of Garvey's
destruction.[4]

The Elder thought association by name with Father Divine and
Bishop Grace, both of whom burst onto the national scene simultaneously with him, threatened his program. He was particularly
of this opinion about Grace, for in Michaux's mind, the Bishop was
preoccupied with accumulating money for the sake of seeing how
much he could collect from members of the House of Prayer for
All People. That greedy behavior, Michaux thought, could dissuade people from giving to the Church of God and other church
groups which they associated with Grace's movement. His conduct also
could make leaders of these groups targets of criminal accusations
and prosecutions akin to those that bedeviled Garvey. Believing
himself to be no lover of money but rather a seeker of funds to
invest and establish a financial base for spreading the Gospel and
for political leverage in a capitalistic and racist society, he publicly
denounced Grace for his seeming predilection to greed. Because
Father Divine was internationally known as a self-styled black
"god" and was identified closely with Daddy Grace by the public,
Michaux denounced Divine as a false prophet. He hoped by this
to enhance his own credibility as a true prophet.

It is ironic that Michaux expended effort combatting name association with Grace and Divine while calling attention to himself as a prophet from God. This image, promoted by him, contributed much to the unwanted association. To many it related him to those cultists because they claimed to be of divine origin and on divine mission. That Michaux was unaware of how he was helping to create this apparent relationship is understandable, for he did not think of himself as having divine nature but as being on a prophetic mission. His mission was to preach and be society's critic versus Divine's and Grace's claims to be conquerors of death, to be God and "Grace," respectively.[5]

Nor were Michaux's antics as showman unrelated to reasons why people often associated him with Divine and Grace. They, too, were showmen, and Grace, like Michaux, held exciting and colorful parades and transformed the sacred ritual of baptism into mass spectacular while Divine sported a "heaven" and presided over sumptuous feasts. Consequently, Michaux's efforts not to be identified with those divines were futile except among members and meticulous outside observers who made conscious distinction in structure, theology, and practices. So there was no cessation in references to Michaux as the "Father Divine of Washington" or in the frequency of confusing him with Daddy Grace.

Conventional writers date the modern black "cult" movement from the late 1920s and 1930s, when there was no Garvey to overshadow them. These writers theorized that mass black migration from southern rural areas to northern urban centers resulted in social and psychological disorientation for many. This problem was compounded by post-World War I economic recession and the onset of the Great Depression. This reasoning subscribes to classical sociological interpretations of cults, interpretations that evolved out of Ernst Troeltsch's church-sect-mysticism typology and of Max Weber's *Sociology of Religion*. Both studied the church from a European perspective. In the United States, scholars interested in the church and influenced by these Europeans were H. Richard Neibuhr, Robert Park, Ernest Burgess, Howard Becker and Elmer Clark, that is, they adhered to a sociological typology. Not all of them discussed cults. Based, however, on a composite of their works on the church and its implications, a stereotypical description of cults has emerged. Members of cults are the oppressed of society and those with psychological needs not fulfilled by church or sect or other social groups. Cults emerge with an ideology that is perceived as the answer to deep psychological needs or as a way out of deprived social situations. They frequently take on dimensions of a revitalization movement to bring about social change. These movements are the breeding ground for prophets and charismatic leaders, and they often fold or splinter after the founder dies. They are also the source of new ideas, creeds, rituals, and involve a considerable portion of the population. Cultists' preachments usually are millennial. Taking cue from classical interpretations more recent scholars concluded that black "cults" were precipitated during the 1920s and 1930s by deplorable social conditions among those who had migrated to northern urban centers.[6]

The rise of black "cults" was not precipitous. Although these new religious assemblies came into prominence in the North after World War I ended, there were viable forerunners, as was Garvey's UNIA in northern cities during the war and early 1920s, in the pre-migration South, as for example, in the late nineteenth century. That was a tragic period, following the Civil War and Reconstruction, of lynchings and manifestations of racial tension, "with a feeble groping in the direction of progress. The law, the courts, the schools, and almost every institution in the South favored the white man. This was white supremacy" after Reconstruction.[7] Many churchmen recognized that something was wrong with organized Christianity that such conditions could exist in this church-rife country. Some concluded that the organized Christian church was a racist institution, void of spiritual vitality that evolves from the presence of the Holy Spirit. In reaction to that institutional racism as well as to religious formalism, several black churchmen seceded from all-black churches and from white-dominated ones to organize Holiness sects that did not cater to race but fought sin and addressed "depressed conditions plaguing Black [folk]. . . . The Holiness movement filtered down to Blacks and gave a definite answer to their troubles and a way out to be found in a highly excitable religious experience. . . . It broke out like wild fire among the masses" in Alabama, Tennessee, Mississippi, Arkansas and other states across the South.[8] Folk in these churches could shout, clap their hands, dance, scream, speak in tongues, prophesy, pray for healing, sing, and create music that would lend itself to cathartic activity. The Church of Christ (Holiness) U.S.A., in which Michaux began his ministry, was among these newly organized nineteenth century assemblies often referred to by sociologists of religion as sects. Michaux belonged to this assembly that was within the Judaeo-Christian tradition, and partly because of his progression from this base did not believe he was a cultist.

Commentators, who would place the precipitous appearance of cults in the North at the time of the Great Depression, are judicious to exclude Michaux from that grouping. His church began in the South among relative prosperity first in 1917, and then in 1919, and in 1921 when he split from the Church of Christ (Holiness). Migrants were among the Elder's first members, but they still lived within proximity to organized southern churches and within familiar, repressive conditions. Many of Michaux's members were not migrants. Those who were, or were migrant workers, had to make psychological adjustments that resulted from moving to a new area within the same geographical region. All of his members experienced mental anguish of having to adjust to rapidly changing society. But no one at that time called him a cultist for addressing himself to all of their needs, physical as well as spiritual.

Problems of social disorientation and repression were not unique to migrants in northern urban areas. Black folk everywhere, and especially those left behind in the South, had problems and anxieties. No one, though, has bothered to raise questions about their anxieties. How, for example, were they affected by their sons', brothers', husbands', lovers', fathers' going off to fight in a war in far-off lands? How did the mass migration of loved ones affect lives of those who stayed behind? How did these already emotionally shocked ones react to post-War recession on farms and in small towns? What would they do to cope with changes in their lives? They had not left familiar surroundings, but reliable conditions had escaped them. Their world had changed. Their lives were uncertain. Many did not want to jostle about alone, trying to make decisions about their lives. They craved stability and assurance that "everything would be all right." So they turned to Holiness and Evangelical groups, which continued to make inroads into southern membership of organized black churches after the war. These less conventional bodies articulated and addressed themselves to needs, fears, longings of masses of black folk in a manner some later likened cultistic. This activity occurred at least a decade before "cults" became prominent in the North. An unknown number of migrants held membership in these Holiness and Evangelical assemblies before leaving the South, as for example, Michaux's members who went North to find work. Joseph Washington expressed this reality when he referred to cults as "the left wing of pentecostal and holiness movements in the South and North."[9]

Let us for a moment concede that Michaux's movement was a cult. It did not occur precipitously. His appeal in Newport News in 1919 is useful illustration that the rehearsal for black "cults" occurred in the predepression South. Beaten down by depressed social conditions and racial oppression, wanting to improve their lives, converts to the Church of Christ (Holiness) U.S.A., that Michaux labored to pastor, caught sight of something inviolable through his preaching: God's love for converts is unchanging, regardless of who dies, migrates, or turns his/her back on you. God is everywhere, all of the time, and hears prayers of righteous ones. You can be part of a caring, sharing, Christian family that will not desert you during critical or bountiful times. Converts made a corresponding "agreement": We will unite with God by joining with Michaux whom we trust will be guided by God in making decisions for us about everyday matters and who will direct us in living so we will never be out of favor with God and each other.

The Elder later carried this same message, that was fashioned in the historical Christian tradition of addressing social and physical as well as spiritual needs, to migrants in the North, beginning in 1924. The same merging of secular and spiritual interests not only was practiced in late nineteenth century assemblies, called sects, but also was as traditional as the original black church on American soil. This early black church's congregation consisted of slaves stealthily gathered in woods around a turned-down pot to hear the preacher tell them how God would deliver them from slavery and other cares and woes. Organized churches in their prosperity and intellectuality later laid aside the black Christian heritage and so were less sensitive to new issues and conditions of black folk than were Michaux and other like-minded religious leaders after the war. Those anxious to label Michaux's movement a cult after it became prominent in several northern cities must take note of its origins, as well as of the fact that no fundamental changes occurred in his doctrine, rituals, or practices when he staked-out northern claims.

Theologians, sociologists, and other commentators create confusion in their rush to define and describe cults in contrast to the organized black church. Yet, they often confess that it is impossible to construct a sociological definition or typology which includes all elements of a cult or sect and excludes all elements of a church. "As social institution, the church-type, sect-type and cult-type each rightly refers to itself as church," one scholar concluded recently. Under the influence, however, of the Troeltsch typology, he attempts to construct an exclusive black cult-typology. He comments, for instance, that cults miss the fullness of the Christian message and usually emphasize Old but ignore the New Testament.[10] Such "indictment" must apply to the black religious experience generally, for historically that experience has been an Old Testament one, filled with charismatic figures. "The essence of slave religion cannot be fully grasped without understanding this Old Testament bias. It is important that Daniel and David and Joshua and Jonah and Moses and Noah, all of whom fill the lines of the Spirituals were delivered in this world and delivered in ways which struck the imagination of slaves." Nat Turner's *Confession* especially is instructive on this point.

> Although Jesus was ubiquitous in the spirituals, it was not invariably the Jesus of the New Testament of whom the slaves sang, but frequently a Jesus transformed into an Old Testament warrior whose victories were temporal as well as spiritual. This transformation is symptomatic of the slaves' selectivity in choosing those parts of the Bible which were to serve as the basis of their religious consciousness.[11]

Michaux was one who related Christianity to the black religious heritage. Although he looked to Old Testament prophets as his role model, his Gospel emphasized Christian principles and pleaded that they be applied to daily living, for example, feeding the hungry, sheltering the evicted, employing the jobless, clothing the naked, accepting the brotherhood of man, dealing with realities of racism and capitalism, encouraging Christian social reform through legislation and presidential mandate. All black preachers who identify with and interpret the black experience inevitably merge spiritual and secular spheres, otherwise they cannot speak to the needs, desires, frustrations, hopes, disappointments and sorrows of their congregations. Traditionally black preachers were interested in the whole man and understood that the black church must be a social agency also—that it must deal with social realities and social uplift. Standing outside the dominant white culture, they had a wide scope of vision out of which to observe and critique the society, bidding it to Higher Order. The central issue for the black preacher traditionally was how men should deal with each other here and now. In this role of social critic, the black preacher was prophet. Nat Turner, Samuel Ringgold Ward, Bishop Henry McNeal Turner, Dr. Martin Luther King, Malcolm X were luminaries in this tradition. An unnumbered host of black preachers, whose contribution is unsung, pursued the same prophetic course. Michaux was within this tradition. Some, who were not where he was theologically or did not appreciate his modus operandi, misunderstood his intentions and to his annoyance called him a cultist.

Several commentators thought they saw cultist traits in authoritarian leadership. Donald Metz, a sociologist, pointed out that cults tended to control and rigidly direct members' lives.[12] Michaux was authoritarian. This aspect of his behavior, however, needs to be analyzed within the context of pastoral administration in churches generally and in black churches specifically. There are pastors in all creeds and denominations who exact obedience to their respective denominations' doctrine and discipline and, moreover, to the pastor's own conscience and inclinations. Otherwise one church would be no different from another and people would have no choices. Accordingly, some pastors dictate members' personal behavior regarding dress, voting, striking on jobs, abortion and birth control, divorce, consumption of alcoholic beverages, and so on. Such strictures are nowhere more vigorously enforced than in the Roman Catholic Church.[13] Many ministers in charge likewise manipulate and monitor church boards to force administrative decisions and procedures in a direction which they deem to be in their churches' best interest.

Members who oppose such strong-armed tactics often leave the church or force the pastors' resignation or exchange. Whenever one is founder of a church, as was Michaux, he normally maintains control and, with only tacit consent of the membership, forges policy. Numerous examples abound in the Baptist church, for instance. W. E. B. Du Bois' reference to black Baptist preachers aptly summarizes this authoritarian posture:

> The preacher is the most unique personality developed by the Negro on American soil. A leader, a politician, an orator, a "boss," an intriguer, an idealist,—all these he is, and ever, too, the centre of a group of men, now twenty, now a thousand in number. The combination of a certain adroitness with deep-seated earnestness, of tact with consummate ability, gave him his preeminence, and helps him maintain it.[14]

So it was with Michaux, and members who opposed consequences of the posture he assumed either left the church or because of their silence tacitly consented to the Elder's directives. But these reflections on the pastor as administrator only partially treat Michaux's authoritarian bent.

The Elder said his "authority" derived from God through "calling" and revelation. Because this claim was based on Michaux's personal and private encounter with God, it was for all practical purposes unchallengeable. Michaux never permitted members to question it, and he refused to respond to external challenges of detractors, asserting that as a prophet of God he was answerable only to God. His members reinforced the validation of his authority over them with testimonies and loyal support of the leadership. Without their validation and support, he would have had no group-approved authority. His "authority" derived from God would have been without license in the ecclesiastical realm had it not been for the Elder's ordination into the Church of Christ (Holiness) U.S.A. Upon this combination of "God-Call," group approval (Church of God), and ecclesiastical sanction (Church of Christ Holiness, U.S.A.), Michaux forged a tyrannical ministry.

Tyranny means the end of creativity indigenous to the body. Michaux's showmanship gave appearance of a new, creative form. But beneath the surface, the movement was hardened at his command rather immediately into "permanent form," without possibility for innovations brought on by spiritual creativity of a vibrant flock and flexible leader amenable to their suggestions. Howard Thurman once wrote in this vein:

> There is a perpetual dilemma which constantly faces any creative movement of the spirit: If the movement is to last, it must somehow be caught and embodied in concrete manifestation. And yet when it is embodied in a concrete form like an organization or an institution, the vitality tends to disintegrate. . . . If the movement survives, it must constantly spill over, break out in a new, fresh way, or it dies [stagnates].[15]

The Church of God was in the structural mold of the organized Negro church, and Michaux did not measurably move it from that form. Furthermore, he so stifled his members' creative freedom that they did not bring innovative ideas and suggestions to him or apply them to church activities. Today, even, they are so inert and void of self-motivation that they await God's "troubling of the water" to cast forth a new leader who can provide program and vibrancy.

Bishop Grace, on the other hand, is called cultist, too, because he was an authoritarian figure. Yet, members had creative license, especially in music. Enough sparks of creativity remained after the bishop's death to keep the movement vibrant. As a result, McCullough, the bishop, could move into the position of leadership, despite objections, and take the movement to new directions, such as political involvement and influence in the Washington, D.C., local government. If Michaux is to be termed a cultist along with Grace because they both were authoritarian, this question must be answered: Are some cults less stultifying than others or than established black churches, and what makes for the different attitudes toward members' freedom to be creative?

When measured beside "cultists," it is evident Michaux's secular and spiritual goals were too steeped in convention and too long ranged to be a "cult" type and attract masses of zealous converts. The white "cultist" Jim Jones, for example, united his followers against immediate threats, greedy capitalists, murderous racists, and he set them about building a "pastoral life" on property they "owned" far from the hoary creatures' machinations. Michaux did not display symbols or evoke images to make members feel immediately threatened or blessed. The cross, various slogans were displayed during special occasions, as for example, the baptizing or other infrequent mass assemblies. At no other times were they visible symbols, nor did members relate to them in day to day introspection, conversation, and testimony as being sacred to doctrine. In the Church of God, God was not even always immediately available. God operated among the righteous according to God's Will and Plan and in God's own time, the Elder explained. There were not even sensational, miraculous healings or demonstrated power over life and death like Father Divine and Daddy Grace claimed.

The Church of God was enigmatic, and to label Michaux a cultist, without reservations, would be an oversimplification. Origin, theology, practices within that church are as suggestive of "sect" as of "cult." Sect is defined as an association of volunteers which seceded from a church (another sect?) because of differences of social and doctrinal origins. This same definition also is applicable to churches in the United States. Scholars inform us that sects espouse stringent moral codes that aim at the sanctity of the individual and strict group discipline. At the center of the sect are doctrine and discipline. The Church of God was, after all, an off-shoot from the Church of Christ (Holiness). Additionally, Michaux drew basic doctrine, practices, and ritual from that Holiness sect and from the established Baptist and Presbyterian denominations. Members who came from those denominations, and many did, systematically pointed out how their former churches failed them. Their doing so in direct contradistinction to ways in which the Church of God fulfilled or did not meet their needs indicates members understood that their assembly had structural and doctrinal relationship to their former churches. According to Moberg eighty percent of all sects previously had been affiliated with established churches. Some followers retained membership in Baptist and other churches while frequenting services at the Church of God; in fact, they sometimes would share with members who were intimates what had happened in their churches that day or week.[16]

At present definitions and descriptions of cults are imprecise and confusing, so that explanations of the term do not clearly show how cults are uniquely different from other religious forms in the black experience. Answers to these questions would be enlightening in this regard. Are cults and sects different religious types? What historical changes have occurred in cult phenomena? or, How are cults today different from ancient ones and those during and immediately following Jesus' lifetime? Do black cults differ from white cults? How do black cults differ from each other? How have black cults changed in relationship to the black organized church since the 1930s?

I am of the opinion that time, cultures, and changing outlooks within groups of people have pressed change (evolution) upon cults—that is if their existence as an autonomous religious type can be validated and clarified.

It is, indeed, incumbent upon theologians and sociologists of religion to clarify what makes cults unique from other religious types. Since Christian history begins with the first century, A.D., and since the early Christian church is often labeled a cult, this is a likely point at which to begin asking questions: Why, for example, is Jesus akin to Father Divine and Bishop Grace? Is it because, like them, He claimed to be divine? He called himself the "Son of God," "The Word made flesh," the "Fore-runner of the Holy Ghost," "One in the Trinity of God the Father, Son and Holy Ghost." Divine claimed to be God, and Grace said he was "Grace," which could save people, at least his members believed this. Is it because on the basis of His divinity, Jesus worked miracles among the people? Is it because He attracted a massive folk following of those who worshipped Him after resurrection and celebrated his crucifixion with communion and his burial with baptism? Should it be, then, that one who claims divine nature on the basis of which he works "miracles" and attracts a mass following of folk that worship him in this life be called a cultist?

Divine, Grace, and Prophet Jones, because of his allegiance to Father Divine in later years, stand outside the Judaeo-Christian experience. Yet, it is precisely because of this that they fit the above conjecture about cults, or some category into which more conventional preachers do not fall. Michaux and several others called cultists do not fit into the conjectured category because they did not diminish the importance of God or Jesus Christ to their followers and claim divinity, or omnipotence. Therefore, such leaders as

Divine and Grace should not be discussed in comparative ways with Michaux or other leaders of religious groups within the Judaeo-Christian fellowship.

Useful definitions and descriptions of religious types within the black religious experience elude us primarily because scholars tend to perpetuate conclusions from dated works of "classicists" with European orientation. A more accurate description of the term cult as it relates to the black experience would be based on the black historical experience within a multi-cultural world. Classical interpretations of institutional life more often than not are inadequate when applied to explain the black experience. It is compelling, therefore, that black scholars, and black theologians in particular, develop definitions and descriptions of black institutional life out of their history. Then when the issue of whether a black religious leader is cultist, sectarian, or churchperson is confronted by the inquisitive, they will have useful standards for discussion.

Categorizing to the contrary, the proper issue to which a biography should be addressed is what dynamics operated to create the life of the individual being investigated? Dynamics in the life of Lightfoot Michaux ranged from simplicity to complexity as he coursed his time span of almost eighty-four years. Continued family references to his being special because of the veil that covered his face at birth caused him to be imbued at an early age with a sense of mission. As a result of this early inspiration, he was driven by the desire to achieve and to be recognized for those achievements, in a way consistent with the Protestant work and reward ethic. Adhering to these motivations he engaged several careers in two fields, business and religion, and he combined the two fields, making a business of religion and business a religion.

Operating small businesses and preaching were, like teaching, traditional professional level vocations among black folk from the nineteenth century on. Because they were frustrated in their efforts to direct primary capitalistic enterprises and were losing customary occupations to white folk and immigrants, black Americans sought to escape economic poverty and to achieve economic independence by opening their own businesses.[17] It is not surprising, therefore, that Michaux, who was reared in a commercial atmosphere, aspired to become a businessman. He was successful in seafood-produce and small construction businesses. Michaux was an opportunist whose business thrived because of World War I. As that conflict wound down and economic recession seemed certain, he accepted the "call" into another respectable career, the ministry, in 1918. The war ended, and he bided time. After virtually all of his patrons left the wartime boomtown and business declined, Michaux returned to Newport News to work with his father and to scout for a new church membership. In 1919, he began a mission within the Church of Christ (Holiness) U.S.A. He stayed with that Holiness group long enough to become a skillful preacher, to acquire familiarity with church administration, to complete the secretive planning for his own church. Then he refused to yield to episcopal privilege and seceded from that body to begin his autonomous church, replete with the legal apparatus for an economic wing. At the time of his secession in 1921, he merged business and religious interests in an incorporated church and building association. This corporation did not mature to any recognizable degree until its spurt of growth during the 1930s.

Michaux was as intuitive, zealous, and opportunistic in his independent ministry as he had been in business. Except for these characteristics he would not have broken into radio at the propitious moment. He was lucky to be broadcasting in the Capital as the decade of the 1930s opened. That was radio's "golden era," and the light-skinned Michaux's theatrical flair caught the nation's attention. He was in a line of entertainers who owed their successes to agonies of the Great Depression and to their ability to amuse the anguished by giving them moments of illusory respite from the crisis. Had it not been for his talents as a showman and his appearance on radio at that time in entertainment history, Michaux would never have become famous, for he was fundamentally no different than the "sect" from which he seceded. His showmanship and interest and involvement in secular as well as religious issues and problems made him seem basically different. Fans marveled about the "show" more than about the Gospel message that the Elder preached after getting their attention. For almost a decade, he touched lives of millions in this country and abroad, black, white, humble masses and exalted dignitaries, via his popular radio broadcast. In using radio and other media to spread the Gospel internationally, he was a forerunner of today's genre of media-oriented preachers, such as Robert Schuller, Jerry Falwell, Pat Robertson and Oral Roberts. The irony is that Michaux, who had international voice, had no national congregational base. He only located churches along the eastern seaboard from Virginia to Pennsylvania and later New York. So except for a handful of sites along the East Coast, he had no local churches that fans could attend or that could help keep his name before the nation of communities. Therefore, the once famous radio evangelist slipped into obscurity after he was dropped from the radio forum.

After he became famous, Michaux was more temperate in demonstrations against racial injustices. During the depression, his attention encompassed national politics and economic injustices. Because of the radio fame, he acquired influence in national political circles and manipulated power cleverly to advance causes which he deemed important. He was momentarily powerful and subject to passionate pursuit of power. That pursuit, as it inevitably must, shaped the life of the pursuer. There are several reasons that Michaux did not abuse power more excessively. He was checked outside as well as inside his church. He was checked via the social tool that helped make him famous, the media. Newspapers released articles that covered suits against him by business associates, investigations of his business affairs and delinquencies, and allusions to the opinion that he engaged in chicanery in business operations and church finance. Notice that his public was observing his behavior and would expose him gave forewarning and caused the Elder to proceed cautiously. This factor alone might have been insufficient. His wife provided additional restraint. Because of her indomitable spirit and proclivity for sharing pressing fears and concerns with members Mrs. Michaux kept her husband on guard. She made everyone aware of her expectations that the Elder should be God's exemplary preacher to a sinful world. With the press on one side and her on the other, Michaux's potential for excessive power abuse was checked. The fact that he was summarily dropped from radio's national and international forum strengthened the force of those two factors. The veracity of Newton's Law was seared on his mind—what goes up must come down. The international pulpit and its accompanying power and fame were snatched suddenly from him, laying foundation for dimunition of his power, power which had contributed to his vulnerability.

Michaux also was vulnerable because he pursued the course of business entrepreneur-preacher. His manuevers in the combined role caused many contemporaries to think he was abusing power and being unethical. He did not, for example, always meet financial obligations. When such difficulties overtook him, Michaux often wielded power among influential Washingtonians in an effort to defer or circumvent obligations. By wielding power, he got suits for back taxes delayed, foreclosures on delinquent mortgages stayed, and he wrangled additional loans from federal lending agencies before paying off arrears on previous loans. Manuevering power often is a matter of course for successful white businessmen, while black ones frequently are destroyed for the audacity to try to play the big financial games. It was to this reality that senators alluded when they wondered if he owed his success in getting federal loans to favoritism. Those privy to Capital gossip were not blind to suggestions that Michaux's financial dealings sometimes bordered on collusion. His acquisition of the Benning Race Track property on which the Mayfair Mansions housing project was built served as an apparent example.

Despite allegations, accusations, and remonstrances, only he determined the extent of his receptivity to caution. Only Michaux could check himself before destruction or prosecution. The Elder was receptive to restraints because he wanted to be a respected preacher, considered amenable to ethical conventions of Christianity, so that members, from whom he required holiness, and the community-at-large would not hold him in contempt. To present this image of respectability while operating as a businessman, he cloaked himself in mysticism. Additionally, he mapped out a plan for self-protection in the event legal authorities interpreted his "bad business judgements" to be criminal deeds or lending and revenue agencies moved to attach his properties. Per the plan, he refused to share detailed information on business matters with members. In fact, even business associates knew little outside specific business they had with him. Since the panorama of business dealings was locked inside him, no one could give the public or its agents information which might not be refutable and thereby might be damaging to Michaux and his agenda. Moreover, because he did not delegate full authority, for any portion of religious and business operations, to any lieutenants, there was no division in leadership and no one other than he was accountable to the public for mistakes. Consequently, Michaux could head off confrontations by appealing to his lack of knowledge about business discretions because he was "a preacher just trying to help his people," or could appeal to powerful Washingtonians without having to bare his soul, and could successfully stall for time and not be anxious that some lieutenant would expose his hand. He did not have concerns, then, that leaders who delegate authority to lieutenants often experience. Garvey had made this mistake when he allowed untrustworthy followers to assume responsibility for managing sales and operation of the Black Starship Line. Ultimately Garvey was held accountable for his lieutenants' mismanagement and judgemental errors. He was deported, and his UNIA disintegrated. Michaux, like other Americans, was informed of Garvey's demise. Since Garvey, who had no traditional institutional base of support and, like Michaux after him, had established an imposing multidimensional operation, there is no reason to believe the Elder did not recognize parallels and learn from Garvey's failings. Michaux's monopoly of authority was not novel. Black leaders customarily were criticized by their followers and associates for failure to delegate responsibility to subordinates.

In other ways Michaux felt vulnerable. He constantly was haunted by the shadow of his past. The demon was his secession from the Church of Christ (Holiness) U.S.A., and this made him feel apprehensive about loyalty of his own members. Remembering that he not only left that former body but took his congregation as well caused the Elder to be on guard so as to try to prevent his own preachers from taking the same action or members from leaving to join other churches. How else can Michaux's insistence on regular church attendance, on no interchurch visitation, and on unswerving loyalty to the Church of God be explained? Before going to Washington, he had not been demanding of members' faithfulness, but the Elder had commanded loyalty by giving them pastoral care.

The faithfulness that he inspired persisted among members until well into the 1950s when second and third generations assumed more control over their own lives and those of their families. They questioned and violated some strictures of the church. They allowed their children to participate in school activities which they had wanted to take part in as youngsters. Members sheltered "erring" children from others' contempt more often than before the 1950s and were less dependent on Michaux's and other members' making decisions about their future and pursuits. Second and third generations were more economically and psychologically independent of the church, and they felt less allegiance to Michaux than their elders had, for the latter ones believed the Elder pointed them to God and helped improve the quality of their lives. Those first generation members, not Michaux, who spent much time traveling around to his several churches from the late 1920s on, had shown their children the "way." The majority of members saw him only two or three hours a week and then he was in a hurry to get to a meeting. All of this added up to the reality that Michaux's control over members' personal lives lessened.

The second generation, though, effectively helped keep changes they began from accelerating more rapidly. By accepting offices and places in church, they became supportive of the established authority, Michaux, helping limit modifications in doctrine and practices and regulations while the Elder lived. That same generation today monopolizes places of power and maintains the status quo except when they deem other action desirable. They try to apply the same tactics of mind control that the Elder devised to entrench his leadership.

Other measures that Michaux took to secure his authority also influence administrative conduct of today's leadership in the Church of God. He did not keep church officers consistently informed on matters pertaining to business. In this he was not unique, for many leaders in all denominations keep members in as much ignorance as possible about their church's operations, especially where business and church politics figure prominently. This is a repressive measure that is designed to keep members from raising meaningful questions about the church's progress or retrogression. These leaders particularly do not want members to raise questions about how business and politics relate to the theology of the denomination or sect.

Like many other church leaders Michaux did not follow business practices and procedural guidelines found in textbooks and his behavior handicapped the succeeding board of directors. They tried to unravel the network of holdings and to untangle the myriad of problems pertaining to delinquent loans, back taxes, Michaux's personal versus church property and terms of contractual agreements after his death. Whether because he needed to protect his interest or not, the Elder had so little respect for members of the board of directors that he did not even list property holdings for their knowledge. After his death, those board members, who already were limited intellectually, were unprepared to be caretakers of the "inheritance," and they soon lost valuable property and profits. Stunned by knowledge that mortgages on Mayfair Mansions were in arrears and payments on back taxes would be staggering, the board grasped at their lawyer's advice. According to their interpretation of his counsel, they could "save" the property by placing it in partnership to him, who would be "general partner," and his associates, who along with the church would be "limited partners," from 1972 to 2017. In the aftermath of their having turned the project over, board members realized, too late, that a few members could have put up several thousand dollars to accomplish the same goal, and moreover, Mayfair Mansions would have remained under direct control of the church. Members knew nothing about the transaction until it was finalized.[18] The next parcel of property which they disposed of in their frustration was the 23.09 beach front acres of the National Memorial land, including access rights to the Colonial Parkway from/onto the church's farm land. They sold that invaluable spread and access rights to the National Park Service for $921,320 and limited use of the beach for fifteen years, from 1978 to 1993.[19]

These trustees might have avoided excessive losses in profit and property if Michaux had provided them with adequate knowledge and experience in the church's business matters. On the other hand, these leaders reflect the general stock among Michaux's converts. They were poor people who dreamed of owning houses, land, and cars but who could not envision themselves as controllers of enterprises that might compete with Colonial Williamsburg and Historic Jamestown in thematic grandeur and significance. That had been

Michaux's dream. Without the vision, these leaders from among the people were not stalwart enough to resist forces that would wrestle valuable claims from them. Michaux's successors were unprepared to accept the challenges that they inherited. Michaux's accomplishments, as the first black man with federally insured loans of over three million dollars, as purchaser of prime real estate on the James River, as provider of the first comfortable rental housing for civil servants and other middle-class black residents in Washington, D.C., pale when one realizes that he did not take the administrative steps necessary to make holdings secure for the "future church," as he termed the youth and their offspring in his last days.

One decade after his death, the Church of God still is in disarray, but is without splits or other signs of imminent disintegration. The financial empire for which Michaux tirelessly labored is all but dissolved. The church and the Michaux family are still at legal odds. That situation promises a more foreboding future since most of the senior Michauxs have died and bequeathed the fight for the inheritance to their more energetic children and grandchildren. Struggles over finance have hampered spiritual development of the church, and no effective leader has emerged to overcome this blighted situation. So these people, who were content to follow Michaux almost blindly while he lived, stumble in dark confusion of the legacy that he left them.

Ironically, despite Michaux's authoritarian posture, the essence of the religious experience in the Church of God also endowed each member with authority. Although they believed the Elder was the main interpreter of the Bible and messenger from God, authority was not his exclusively. Anyone filled with the Holy Spirit could be used by God to express a vision or deliver a message, but the Elder had to give it sanction before most members would accept that message as prophetic. Preachers in the Church of God were not recognized to have any more authority than other members. These preachers, in fact, have not been able to persuade members to believe they are professionally competent or divinely inspired, and that is one reason no one of them has emerged as leader. Michaux's neglecting to train and ordain them helped place them in this bind while making him feel less threatened in his leadership.

The Elder's ministry consisted of three distinct phases. During the pre-Washington years (1919-27), he zealously preached to all people about the brotherhood of man, the salvation of God, lovingly pastored his members, and organized his church for expansion. Second, upon becoming famous in the radio ministry, he tried to practice what he preached by applying Christian principles to social ills and making political recommendations. Finally, after the radio ministry declined, he concentrated on making the business of the church successful, was self-aggrandizing, and his preaching and application of the Gospel took secondary position.

Like the church so inextricably identified with him, he was a complex personality, abounding in paradoxes. He was a Fundamentalist-type preacher of the Gospel with a "New Thought" interpretation. He was powerful and vulnerable and inscrutable, nontrusting even of those he called saints. He was traditional and innovative, conventional and unorthodox. He was paternalistic and unapproachable. He was indefatigable and restless but also serene in appearance. He was interested in racial problems but was not a man of race. He was capitalistic, espousing principles of Christian communism. He was a mission-oriented egotist. He was practical and visionary. He exacted high morality of members while engaging in questionable business practices himself. He needed the church but never failed to emphasize its dependence on him. Members were in awe of him. Contemporaries outside the membership looked upon him askance. Few were supportive of his programs other than the Baptizing. He, who had risen from peddling fish to "counseling presidents," was an inspiration for poor, lower-class members in search of upward mobility. He was an unbelievable businessman, a showman, the "Happy Am I Preacher."

Notes

Author's Note: My relationship to the members of the Church of God has been very special. My grandparents joined the church early in its history, and my parents were reared within its body. I was an active member of the church until I was about fifteen, and my membership did not end until some years later. Therefore, much of the information in this book is based on firsthand observations.

I conducted all of the interviews and participated in all of the discussions and conversations referred to in this book. These were numerous, informal, and not taped except where specified. Most took place in Newport News and Hampton, Virginia, over the span of two decades. Since the Church of God members and ex-members that I interviewed requested anonymity, I refer to them here simply as members. Because I knew many of these people very well, they were willing to share their thoughts and reminiscences generously with me, for which I am grateful.

INTRODUCTION

1. "Sixty Minutes," CBS Television, Sunday, November 19, 1978.
2. Frank Rasky, "Harlem's Religious Zealots," *Negro Digest* 8 (March 1950), pp. 52–62.

3. E. Franklin Frazier, *The Negro Church of America* (New York: Schocken Books, 1964), pp. 60–61.

4. Marcus Boulware, *The Oratory of Negro Leaders: 1900–1968* (Westport, Ct.: Negro Universities Press, 1969), pp. 204–6.

5. Roscoe Lewis, *The Negro in Virginia* (Hampton, Va.: Hampton Institute Press, 1940), pp. 256, 346.

6. Chancellor Williams, "The Socio-Economic Significance of the Store-Front Church Movement in the United States Since 1920" (Ph.D. diss., American University, 1949), chap. 3.

CHAPTER 1

1. Eugene Genovese, *Roll, Jordan, Roll* (New York: Random House, Pantheon Books, 1974), p. 218.

2. Michaux, who said he "loved old people but hated old age," never told his age, so dates given posthumously conflict. This date for his birth is based on obituaries in *New York Times* and other East Coast newspapers, October 21, 1968, and on tombstone inscriptions at Michaux's grave-site in Pleasant Shade Cemetary, Newport News, Virginia. In conflict with this date is one inscribed on a bronze bust of the Elder at the entrance of the church's museum in Jamestown, Virginia. It carries 1883–1968 for the span of his life.

3. Based on author's discussions with Michaux's sister, Mrs. Jenny McRae, 1969–70 and 1972 in Newport News, Va. She died in late 1976. (Hereafter cited as author's conversations with Mrs. McRae.) Also from *Washington Post* (Washington, D.C.), October 13, 1956, and years of intermittent conversations with elderly residents in Newport News and Hampton who were members of the Church of God. (Hereafter cited as author's discussions with church members.)

4. From author's discussions with Mrs. McRae and with elderly members of the church.

5. Ibid.

6. From author's taped interview in Hampton, Va., in January 1972, with an employee in Michaux's World War I seafood business. Tapes in author's possession. (Hereafter cited as author's interview with seafood business employee.)

7. Information about Michaux as a child and young adult comes from his sermons and pulpit talks with members, from author's conversations with Mrs. McRae, and from *Washington Post* (Washington, D.C.), October 13, 1956. Having found his quitting school early to be a mistake, even something of a handicap, he eventually hired tutors after becom ng famous as radio evangelist.

8. See W. T. Stauffer, "The Old Farms," *William and Mary Quarterly*, 2nd Ser., 14 (July 1934): 203-15; Mrs. Lewis T. Jester, *Newport News, Virginia, 1607-1960* (Newport News, 1961), pp. 3, 110, 115-16, 120, 122-27; Alexander C. Brown, ed., *Newport News' 325 Years* (Newport News, 1946), pp. 76, 80-90, 133.

9. Based on Michaux's reminiscences from the pulpit, for which the author was present; author's interview with seafood business employee; and a Saint Timothy Church book of minutes of church meetings which the Elder, as secretary-treasurer, kept in his own handwriting and signed during the war (book of minutes of church meetings in possession of a Saint Timothy Church member, in Newport News, Va.).

10. From author's conversations with Mrs. McRae. After her sisters-in-law were grown, Mrs. Michaux often asked members to let their daughters come live with her. Several young women stayed in her home for a number of years, traveling with her and helping to keep her company. In 1956, the Elder brought a young Eskimo girl from Alaska. She was about nine and was called Ieeda Martin.

11. From author's interview with seafood business employee and from author's discussions with church members.

12. John Hope Franklin, *From Slavery to Freedom* (New York: Alfred A. Knopf, 1974), pp. 333-53, contains a discussion of black participation in World War I.

13. Michaux talked about his World War I ventures in *Minutes of the Church of God Elders and Deacons Quarterly Meetings*, July 4, 1957. Xeroxed copy in author's possession. (Hereafter cited as *Minutes*.) See also *Daily Press* (Newport News), February 15, 1919, 11, and author's interview with seafood business employee.

14. *Sunday Star* (Washington, D.C.), July 10, 1938, A-3; *Seven Churches* (Washington, D.C.), February 1950, p. 3. (The latter is a Church of God publication, hereafter cited as *Seven Churches*.)

15. Based on author's interview with seafood business employee. On black middle-class and seminary training see, for example, Frazier, *Negro Church*, p. 17.

16. Information taken from biographical sketch in Harry A. Ploski and Roscoe C. Brown, Jr., eds., *The Negro Almanac* (New York: Bellwether Publishing Company, 1967), p. 800, and from discussions with members who heard Michaux talk about this incident. Material on Bishop C. P. Jones is from Frank S. Meade, *Handbook of Denominations in the United States* (New York: Abingdon Press, 1965), p. 71, and C. Eric Lincoln, *The Black Experience in Religion* (Garden City, N.Y.: Doubleday, Anchor Press, 1974), p. 208.

17. From interview with Handy's nephew (Norfolk, Va., Spring 1972), author's conversations with members of Saint Timothy Church (Newport News, Va., Spring 1972), author's discussions with church members, and from Ethel L. Williams, comp., *Biographical Directory of Negro Ministers* (New York: Scarecrow Press, 1965), p. 157.

18. *Daily Press*, February 15, 1919, p. 11. The caption read "Hopewell City Now Deserted."

19. Jester, *Newport News*, pp. 145–46.

20. From author's interview with seafood business employee.

21. Ibid.

22. Accounts of the Church of God's beginnings are found in almost all of the church's literature, for example, *Seven Churches*. Also see Jester, *Newport News*, p. 141. A man in a 1919 photograph in the *Shipyard Bulletin*, Spring 1971, bears strong resemblance to Deacon Charlie Grant of Newport News.

23. Based on author's discussions with church members.

24. Jester, *Newport News*, p. 141. Information about members is based on author's discussions with church members.

25. Frazier, *Negro Church*, p. 34.

26. W. E. B. Du Bois, *The Negro Church*, from the Atlanta University Conferences (Atlanta: Atlanta University Press, 1903).

27. Pauline Lark, ed., *Sparks from the Anvil of Elder Michaux* (Washington, D.C.: Happy News Publishing Company, 1950), p. 115.

28. From author's discussions with church members.

29. H. Richard Neibuhr, *Social Sources of Denominationalism* (New York: World Publishing Company, 1965); and Lincoln, *Black Experience in Religion*, p. 208. Michaux never discussed his secession apparently because he did not want to give his preachers, who might hold similar intentions, comfort or easy rationale. He continuously cautioned them not to split the church. I was directed to the fact of secession by hearing elderly members mention their having attended a convention with Michaux. Since the Church of God had no gathering that was referred to as "convention," I asked questions and learned that Michaux had, indeed, previously been affiliated with another church. Information about this comes from author's discussions with church members of both the Church of God and Saint Timothy in Newport News where he was an officer. See also O. B. Cobbins, ed., *History of Church of Christ (Holiness), U.S.A.* (New York: Vantage Press, 1966), pp. 37–39, on these early conventions.

30. *Pictorial Review* (Washington: Happy News Publishing Company), August 1941, p. 37. Hereafter cited as *Pictorial Review*.

31. From author's interview in 1972 with a woman who was an active member in the Prayer Band in the Newport News Church and from author's discussions with church members.

32. *Times Herald* (Newport News), October 16, 1922; and *Daily Press,* October 17, 1922. Members who participated in the early morning march and were arrested shared memories of the event with the author.

33. From author's conversations with Mrs. McRae and author's discussions with church members.

CHAPTER 2

1. Bernhard W. Andersen, *Understanding the Old Testament* (Englewood Cliffs, N.J.: Prentice-Hall, 1975), p. 226.

2. Ibid., p. 227.

3. "Happy Am I Preacher: Elder Michaux," Savoy Record Company, Inc., ca. 1962. Hereafter cited as *Savoy Record Album.*

4. These pertained to national politics: The National Recovery Act, the supreme court packing, and President Truman's election. See chap. 3 on Michaux and the presidents.

5. *Minutes,* January 1956.

6. *Daily Press,* May 12, 1923.

7. From author's discussions with church members.

8. William E. Leuchtenburg, ed., *The Unfinished Century: America Since 1900* (Boston, Mass.: Little, Brown, 1973).

9. From author's remembrance of Michaux's pulpit talks in the Church of God, and author's discussions with church member who attended the klansmen's church with Michaux. In the late 1960s, the author observed that this man's daughter, who was called Sister Katherine, was still active in the Baltimore church.

On blacks preaching to whites, see Miles Mark Fisher, "Organized Religion and the Cults," *Crisis,* January 1937, pp. 9–10, and Henry Mitchell, *Black Preaching* (New York: Harper and Row, 1970), pp. 65–94.

10. June P. Guild, *Black Laws in Virginia* (1936; reprint ed., New York: Negro Universities Press, 1969), pp. 148–49, for text of Public Assembly Law.

11. "Elder Michaux," *Our World* 2 (January 1950): 46; *Courier Magazine Section* (Pittsburgh: February 28, 1953); Williams, "Store-Front Church Movement," p. 90.

12. From author's discussions with church members. Quotation is based on Matt. 13:57.

13. *Sunday Star*, July 19, 1938.

14. *Commissioners Minutes LIV, Part 2* (Washington, D.C.: June 20, 1933), p. 787; *Amsterdam News* (New York, September 29, 1934).

15. Spence Miller, "Radio and Religion," *Annals of the American Academy* 177 (January 1935): 135–37.

16. *Evening Star* (Washington, D.C.), July 11, 1938 and *Sunday Star*, July 10, 1938.

17. Constance M. Green, *The Secret City: A History of Race Relations in the Nation's Capital* (Princeton, N. J.: Princeton University Press, 1967), pp. 213–15.

18. *Evening Star*, July 11, 1938.

19. *Journal and Guide* (Norfolk), April 28, 1934; *Evening Star*, July 11, 1938; *Sunday Star,*July 10, 1938; *Amsterdam News*, September 29, 1934.

20. *Savoy Record Album*, and *Pictorial Review*, p. 22.

21. "Nations Are Rising Against Nations; Look Up the End Is Nigh," a sermon by Elder Michaux, November 4, 1956. Quotations from sermons are taken from typed transcripts unless otherwise noted.

22. Untitled sermon by Elder Michaux, October 8, 1939.

23. *Pictorial Review*, p. 9.

24. "Nations Are Rising," sermon by Elder Michaux, November 4, 1956.

25. "Revised Standard Version of the Bible," sermon by Elder Michaux, n.d.

26. *Savoy Record Album.*

27. Untitled sermon by Elder Michaux, October 8, 1939.

28. Williams, "Store-Front Church Movement," p. 74.

29. *Pictorial Review*, p. 4; "Resurrection of the Saints," sermon by Elder Michaux, n.d.; *Minutes*, November 1955.

30. Clyde E. Fant, Jr., and William M. Pinson, Jr., eds., *Twenty Centuries of Great Preaching* IV and VI (Waco, Tx.: Word Books Publishers, 1976).

31. Information on Michaux's tutors is from two ministers once associated with the Church of God who often were the Elder's companions. Tape of one interview (Newport News, Va., March 1972) in author's possession; notes for second interview (Washington, D.C., December 1978) in author's possesson.

32. Interview conducted on February 3, 1972, in Newport News.

33. *Washington Post*, October 28, 1934.

34. *Minutes*, January 1957.

35. "Nations Are Rising," sermon by Elder Michaux, November 4, 1956.

36. "Resurrection of the Saints," sermon by Elder Michaux, n.d.

37. "Second Front in Harlem; Elder Michaux and His Choir," *Time* 40 (December 1942), pp. 74–76, and untitled sermon by Elder Michaux, October 8, 1939.

38. "Nations Are Rising," sermon by Elder Michaux, November 4, 1956.

39. *Time* 40 (December 1942), p. 74.

40. "Nations Are Rising," sermon by Elder Michaux, November 4, 1956.

41. Ibid.

42. Lark, *Sparks from the Anvil*; and many news clippings in the Washington, D.C., public library in the file on Michaux.

Henry Mitchell discusses features of black sermons in *Black Preaching*, pp. 156–68.

43. *Pictorial Review*, p. 59.

44. *Journal and Guide*, April 28, 1934, and *Happy News*, Christmas-News Year's Edition, 1933–34. This was the church's monthly tabloid, which was first published in 1933 and is still published.

45. Ibid., and Winifred Phillips, Programme Correspondence Section, BBC to author, October 19, 1971.

46. *Amsterdam News*, September 29, 1934, and *Happy News*, November 1933.

47. *Happy News*, Christmas-New Year's Edition, 1933–34, December 1936, and January 1937.

48. *Happy News*, November 1933; *Washington Herald* (Washington, D.C.), May 1, 1933; *Washington Tribune* (Washington, D.C.), April 5 and September 29, 1934; *Washington Daily News*, September 22, 1934; *Washington Star*, March 6, 1933, provide information on his programs' content. Also from *Pictorial Review* and the the Elder's members.

49. *Journal and Guide*, April 28, 1934, and *Happy News*, September 1935. Letter from Mrs. Mamie Eisenhower's office to author, November 23, 1971.

50. *Washington Star*, March 6, 1933 and September 22, 1941.

51. Williams, "Store-Front Church Movement," p. 58.

52. *Washington Sentinel* (Washington, D.C.), January 6, 1934.

53. *Washington Post*, October 28, 1934, and *Pictorial Review*, p. 59.

54. *Journal and Guide*, April 28, 1934.

55. Fisher, "Organized Religion and the Cults," p. 10, and *Pictorial Review*, pp. 41–51.

56. *Happy News*, March 1934.

57. *Journal and Guide*, December 15, 1934; *Evening Star*, July 11, 1938; and *Pictorial Review*.

58. *Washington Tribune*, September 29, 1934; and *Washington Daily News*, September 22, 1934. Also see Thomas Cripps, *Slow Fade to Black: The Negro in American Film, 1900–1942* (New York: Oxford University Press, 1977), p. 381.

59. *Washington Tribune*, September 29, 1934; *Happy News*, June 1935; and *Sunday Star*, July 10, 1938.

60. *Happy News*, December 1936 and January 1937. Also from Winifred Phillips to author, October 19, 1971; and *Pictorial Review* (letter from Crum to Michaux, September 30, 1936), p. 6.

61. *Evening Star*, July 12, 1938.

62. *Washington Post*, October 28, 1934, and Fisher, "Organized Religion and the Cults."

63. Chap. 3 gives details on Michaux's fund-raising.

64. Verification of the termination of broadcasts to the British Empire by Winifred Phillips in letter to author, October 19, 1971.

65. From author's observations of church photographs.

66. *Seven Churches*, pp. 21, 23; and Michaux's obsequies in the *Daily Press* (Newport News, Va., October 21, 1968); and the church's eulogy, a copy of which the author possesses.

67. Film on that trip was in possession of Brother Jackson, a photographer in the Washington church, who accompanied Michaux; and from Michaux's comments made in the church at Newport News upon his return from that trip. As remembered by the author, who was present on that occasion.

CHAPTER 3

1. Williams, "Store-Front Church Movement," pp. 72, 74; and *Evening Star*, July 13, 1938.

2. *Happy News*, January 1953.

3. Andersen, *Understanding the Old Testament*, p. 231.

4. Green, *Secret City*, chap. 10.

5. *Evening Star*, July 13, 1938.

6. Williams, "Store-Front Church Movement," p. 72; *Courier Magazine*, February 28, 1953; Roger Daniels, *The Bonus March, An Episode of the Great Depression* (Westport, Conn.: Greenwood Press, 1971), p. 322.

7. Pelham Glassford, Chief of the D.C. Police, to Michaux, June 14, 1932, Glassford Papers, UCLA Library, Los Angeles.

8. *Evening Star*, July 13, 1938; and Williams, "Store-Front Church Movement," p. 72.

9. Ibid.

10. *Pictorial Review*, p. 46.

11. *New York Tribune*, March 11, 1951.

12. *Pictorial Review*, p. 58; and *Courier Magazine*, February 28, 1953, p. 5.

13. *Happy News*, November 1933; and *Journal and Guide*, April 28, 1934.

14. *Pictorial Review*, p. 58.

15. Ibid., and *Happy News*, 1934–36.

16. *Pictorial Review*, p. 62; and from Williams, "Store-Front Church Movement," pp. 78–79.

17. *Happy News*, July 1934.

18. Williams, "Store-Front Church Movement," p. 73.

19. Ibid., p. 74.

20. *Happy News*, February 1934.

21. Bernard Garnett, "Elder Called 'Most Unbelievable Businessman in History,' " *Jet* 36 (April 24, 1969), pp. 20–25.

22. *Minutes*, January 1956.

23. Based on author's discussions with a member of Michaux's church who participated in the "Common Plan."

24. From author's discussions with church members. This man bought several houses after leaving the "Common Plan."

25. Based on discussions with a member of the church whose family was involved in the incident.

26. Based on author's discussions with church members; and *Daily News*, February 9, 1933.

27. *Minutes*, January 1956.

28. Based on author's discussions with church members.

29. *Evening Star*, July 13, 1938; and *Pictorial Review*, pp. 10–11.

30. Ibid. Michaux never shared publicly his reactions to President Roosevelt's diplomatic recognition of Russia in 1933.

31. Otis Graham, the New Deal historian, writes about Hugh Johnson in the *Unfinished Century*, p. 373.

32. *Evening Star*, July 13, 1938.

33. Michaux to Roosevelt, March 19, 1936, Roosevelt Papers, p. 1.

34. "High: Roosevelt's 'Spokesman Disowned,' " *Newsweek* 9 (February 13, 1937), p. 14; "Democrat's St. Paul," *Time 27*; (June 1, 1936), p. 27; Donald R. McCoy, "The Good Neighbor League and the Presidential Campaign of 1936," *Western Political Quarterly* 13 (December 1960): 1012; and *Time* (May 4, 1936), p. 14.

35. *Evening Star*, July 13, 1938. Michaux had operated a charitable organization during the Great Depression under the name of Good Neighbor League, a name derived from Hoover's "Good Neighbor" speech.

36. *New York Times*, September 3, 1936.

37. *New York Times*, September 4, 1936; McCoy, "Good Neighbor League," p. 1015; Stanley High, *Roosevelt—and Then?* (New York: Harper and Brothers Publisher, 1937), p. 201; *Pictorial Review*, p. 28. (That Madison Square Garden rally was held on September 21, 1936.)

38. See *Pictorial Review*, which gives some indication of the measure of Michaux's Caucasian following at the height of his popularity in the 1930s.

39. *Happy News*, October 1936 and July 1938.

40. Elizabeth Ross Haynes presents Wright's biography in *The Black Boy of Atlanta* (Boston, Mass.: House of Edinboro, 1952). See also *La Releve* (Port-au-Prince, Haiti), January 1937; and *Happy News*, February 1935, for more information on Wright and his interest in Haitian coffee.

41. *Foreign Relations of the United States: Diplomatic Papers, 1937* 5 (Washington, D.C., 1954), pp. 529-31.

42. Rayford W. Logan, *Haiti and the Dominican Republic* (New York: Oxford University Press, 1968), p. 145; and Hans Schmidt, *The United States' Occupation of Haiti, 1915-1934* (New Brunswick, N.J.: Rutgers University Press, 1971), p. 207.

43. Ibid.

44. Sumner Welles, Under Secretary of State, to Marvin McIntyre, Assistant Secretary to President Roosevelt, February 26, 1937, Roosevelt Papers.

45. Ibid.

46. Ibid.

47. Ibid.

48. *Whetstone* (Durham: North Carolina Mutual Life Insurance Company Newsletter), May 1937.

49. *Happy News*, February 1935; and Fisher, "Organized Religion and the Cults," p. 9.

50. Gordon to Welles, April 19, 1937, Roosevelt Papers.

51. Ibid.

52. From author's taped interview with Emmanuel C. Wright, the major's son, Philadelphia, November 1971; taped discussions with the former Field Representative of Michaux's church in Newport News, March 2, 1972, and *Whetstone*, May 1937.

53. *Pictorial Review*, pp. 34-36; *Minutes*, July 4, 1958, and July 4, 1959. Michaux called that area the National Memorial Beach.

54. *Daily Press*, July 8, 1937.

55. *Washington Tribune*, March 29, 1937; and *Daily Press*, July 8, 1937.

56. Ibid.; Floyd Flickinger, Superintendent Colonial National Historical Park, to Director Cammerer, July 15, 1937, with reference to a November 9, 1936 letter from Demaray to Michaux. Department of the Interior Correspondence, File No. 610, Box 118, National Archives.

57. *Daily Press*, June 23, 1937, July 3, 1937, July 22, 1937; and *Newport News Star*, July 31, 1937.

58. *Daily Press*, September 11, 1937.

59. Flickinger to Cammerer, July 15, 1937, National Archives.

60. Cammerer to Flickinger, July 16, 1937, National Archives.

61. *Journal and Guide*, November 13, 1937.

62. "Daddy Grace's Cuban Paradise," *Ebony* 9 (November 1953), p. 86.

63. *Journal and Guide*, November 13, 1937.

64. Parke Rouse, Jr., "Happy Am I," *The Commonwealth* 32 (July 1965), p. 32.

65. Based on letter from Owens to Secretary Ickes, Department of the Interior, December 28, 1939, and Department employee Moskey to Rader, October 14, 1940. Also see Owens to Ickes, October 14, 1939. Smith, who agreed to give Owens twenty percent of the sale price, discharged Owens and dealt directly with the department. National Archives.

66. Owens to Ickes, July 24, 1939, National Archives.

67. Owens to Demaray, September 25, 1939; and Demaray to Owens, September 29, 1939, National Archives.

68. Owens to Chapman, October 25, 1939, National Archives.

69. Owens to Ickes, December 8, 1939, National Archives.

70. See Park Service correspondence, February 1940 to May 1940, National Archives.

71. Memo, Attorney General's Office to Department of Interior, Septmember 1945, Department of Interior Correspondence, National Archives.

72. From author's discussions with church members and members of the Board of Directors, and from author's own observations.

CHAPTER 4

1. Address by Michaux, *Official Proceedings of the Democratic National Convention*, Chicago, July, 1940, pp. 203-4.

2. Michaux to Roosevelt, July 21, 1940. Roosevelt Papers.

3. Rouse, "Happy Am I," p. 32.

4. Information on Goldberg and Michaux film versus the United States is from Thomas R. Cripps based on his research in this area for his book, *Slow Fade to Black*.

5. White House memo, January 20, 1948, Truman Papers, Harry S Truman Library, Independence, Missouri.

6. *Washington Post*, January 23, 1948.

7. From author's discussions with church members.

8. Michaux to Eisenhower, June 20, 1948. Copy to Truman, Truman Papers.

9. White House memo, June 23, 1948, Truman Papers.

10. Michaux to Matthew Connelly, Secretary to Truman, July 1948, Truman Papers. Truman penned a memo stating that the autographed cartoon was to be placed in his personal collection.

11. Harry S Truman, *Memoirs: Years of Trial and Hope*, II (Garden City, N.Y.: Doubleday and Company, 1956), p. 181.

12. From undated program script found among remnants of Michaux's personal papers and based on author's discussions with church members.

13. Henry Lee Moon, *The Balance of Power* (Garden City, N.Y.: Doubleday and Company, 1949), and also see Franklin, *From Slavery to Freedom*, p. 613.

14. Jules Abels, *Out of the Jaws of Victory* (New York: Henry Holt and Company, 1959), pp. 293-95.

15. Moon, *Balance of Power*.

16. Michaux's obsequies from the Church of God; a triumphal song entitled, "Tru-Man," written and published by Michaux in 1949; and from author's discussions with church members who had observed this reaction from other members on their jobs and in church.

17. *Pictorial Review*, p. 46.

18. General Eisenhower to Michaux, January 6, 1945. Eisenhower Papers, Dwight D. Eisenhower Library, Abilene, Kansas.

19. Eisenhower to Michaux, September 11, 1945, Eisenhower Papers.

20. Dwight D. Eisenhower, *The White House Years: Mandate for Change, 1953-1956* (Garden City, N.Y.: Doubleday and Company, 1963), pp. 4-5.

21. Michaux to Eisenhower, June 30, 1948, Eisenhower Papers.

22. Michaux to Mrs. Eisenhower, October 26, 1954, Eisenhower Papers.

23. Michaux to Shanley (Counsel to the president), September 6, 1956; Eisenhower to Michaux, September 6, 1956; and White House memo, Eisenhower Papers.

24. From a newspaper clipping, *n.d.* or name or paper; clipping is in author's possession.

25. Michaux to Shanley, September 18, 1956, Eisenhower Papers.

26. Michaux to Shanley, November 3, 1956, Eisenhower Papers; and from interview with Elder Rhodes' sister, who lives in Detroit, February 1979.

27. From a radio sermon, October 28, 1956, which was found in the Eisenhower Papers. Michaux did not live to see Nixon elected after he previously had lost a presidential election to John Kennedy.

28. Ibid.

29. *Savoy Record Album* jacket; *Happy News*, June 1959.

30. *Minutes*, January 1960.

31. Haynes, *Black Boy of Atlanta*, p. 137.

32. *Happy News*, October 1961; and from *Souvenir Program* (a Church of God publication), dated September 10, 1961, hereafter referred to as *Souvenir Program*.

33. From author's conversation with Louis Michaux in Oxonhill, Maryland, Summer 1972.

34. *Happy News*, October 1963.

35. Copy of Open Letter, *Happy News*, January 1965.

36. Ibid.

37. Rouse, "Happy Am I," *Commonwealth*, p. 33.

38. From author's discussions with church members, across the field of Churches of God, who participated, and based on author's own observations.

39. *Pictorial Review*, p. 63.

40. Frank Rasky, "Harlem's Religious Zealots," *Negro Digest* 8, March 1950, p. 57.

CHAPTER 5

1. From Michaux's pulpit talks and from author's discussions with church members and folk in the communities where there are Churches of God.

2. From author's discussions with church members and based on author's own observations.

3. From author's discussions with church members who participated in that first ten-day fast.

4. Based on author's own observations and author's discussions with church members.

5. Early in 1960 a special forty-day fast was held to celebrate the fortieth anniversary of the Church of God; see *Minutes*, April 1960.

For attention given to presidents during these periods of fasting and praying, refer to libraries for Presidents Roosevelt, Truman, and Eisenhower; also see *Minutes*.

For more complete text of conversion testimonies, see William James, *The Varieties of Religious Experience* (New York: Macmillan Company, 1961), pp. 202–3.

6. Based on author's observations over several years of members' testimonies in all-night prayer meetings and the week or so that followed. For "state of assurance" expression, see James, *Varieties of Religious Experience*, p. 198.

7. *Happy News; Minutes;* Church of God brochures and program booklets, and author's own observations.

8. *Seven Churches*, pp. 1, 26.

9. From author's taped discussions with the Field Representative, a former member who initiated and organized these two activities, Newport News, May 2, 1972.

10. Refer to David O. Moberg, *The Church as a Social Institution* (Englewood Cliffs, N.J.: Prentice-Hall, 1964), p. 83, for general discussion on the extent of offices and positions in churches and "sects."

11. Ibid.

12. Benjamin E. Mays and Joseph W. Nicholson, *The Negro's Church* (New York: Institute of Social and Religious Research, 1933), p. 231.

13. *Minutes of the Commissioners of the District of Columbia*, June 20, 1933, LIV, pt. 2, 783, National Archives. See also *Fiftieth Anniversary Brochure;* and *Pictorial Review*, pp. 49–50.

14. From *Washington Post*, October 28, 1934; and author's own observations over several years.

15. *Fiftieth Anniversary Brochure; Washington Post*, October 28, 1934 and October 13, 1956; and author's own observations over several years.

16. "Elder Michaux," *Our World* 5 (January 1950): 47.

17. *Richmond News Leader* (Richmond, Virginia), July 12, 1960.

18. From author's discussions with employees of Michaux's church.

19. See Michaux's obsequies from the church, October 27, 1968; *Pictorial Review*, pp. 49–50; and based on author's own observations over several years.

20. *Fiftieth Anniversary Brochure* and author's own observations over several years.

21. *Minutes*, July 1959, and author's own observations over several years and across the field of churches.

22. *Fiftieth Anniversary Brochure* and author's own observations.

23. *New York Times*, October 1, 1934; *Journal and Guide*, February 26, 1938; *Daily Press*; and *Times Herald*, during summer months, 1934–68.

24. Based on photographs in *Pictorial Review*; Michaux's obsequies; *Fiftieth Anniversary Brochure*; and author's own observations.

25. From the author's interview at Hampton Institute in November 1971 with a retired U.S. Army Colonel and instructor at Hampton Institute. He once was a stand-in for a general at a Michaux revival, also from conversations with members, and author's own observations.

26. *Washington Tribune*, September 7, 1933.

27. *Happy News*, August, September, October 1933–67; *Pictorial Review*, p. 60; news clippings in the Washington Public Library; and H. Richard Niebuhr, *Social Sources of Denominationalism*, pp. 12–13, where he discusses celebration of this sacrament among "sects" and denominations.

28. From author's observations over several years of Baptizings; *Pictorial Review*, p. 60; and *Washington Star*, September 30, 1940, and September 19, 1949.

29. Melville J. Herskovits, *The Myth of the Negro Past* (Boston, Mass.: Beacon Press, 1958), pp. 232–34.

30. "Second Front in Harlem; Elder Michaux and His Choir," *Time* 40 (December 21, 1942), p. 76; *Annual Baptizing Souvenir Program*, 1949; and *Pictorial Review*, p. 23.

It was not unusual for evangelists to dress in white. Aimee McPherson, for example, was a colorful religious leader who sailed into the Norfolk, Virginia, port upon her return from Europe in 1933 dressed completely in white, even wearing white makeup. See *Time Herald*, March 21, 1970, p. 9.

31. *Washington Post*, October 13, 1956.

32. Ibid., and *Annual Baptizing Souvenir Program*, 1966.

33. "WJSV," *Time* 66 (October 3, 1955), p. 40.

34. *Washington Daily News*, September 22, 1934; *Washington Star*, September 17, 1949. In *Our World*, ca. August 1950, there is a baptizing souvenir insert from Michaux's church program booklet. Copy in author's possession.

35. *Happy News*, September 1933–68, and *Baptizing Souvenir Program*, 1966.

36. "Second Front in Harlem," *Time* 40 (December 1942), p. 76.

37. In the Washington, D.C., public library, see the large volume of clippings in the file on Michaux. See, for example, clippings from *Washington Star*, September 21, 1947, and September 19, 1949; *Washington Post*, September 30, 1940, and August 23, 1943; and *Washington Afro-American*, September 1950.

38. *Happy News*, October 1946 and 1947; "Mass Negro Baptizing," *Life* 26 (April 4, 1949), pp. 24–26; *Washington Tribune*, September 29, 1934; and *Washington Daily News*, September 22, 1934.

39. *Happy News*, 1933–68; *Washington Star*, September 22, 1941; and author's conversations with friends and colleagues from Howard University who attended the church until 1962.

40. *Washington Star*, July 1938 and October 1948. Also from author's own observations over several years.

41. Bernard Garnett, " 'Most Unbelievable Black Businessman in History,' " *Jet*, April 24, 1969, p. 24.

42. *Washington Post*, October 13, 1956.

43. See, for example, Richard La Coste, "Elder Michaux, 'Happy Am I' Preacher," *Courier Magazine*, February 28, 1953; and Boulware, *Oratory of Negro Leaders*, pp. 204–6.

CHAPTER 6

1. *Minutes*, January 1954.

2. See *Minutes*, November 1955.

3. From author's own observations over several years. That Michaux recognized most members by name or family resemblance indicates the

high degree of intrachurch marriages and the low infusion of new members after each church was founded.

4. *Minutes*, April 1956.

5. Members, such as Deacons F. D. Raney and Rudolph Jones, often referred to Michaux in testimonies as "a prophet in the last day," or "the last prophet." Such veneration continued in all of the seven churches and branches after his death but decreased when problems he left were not soon resolved.

6. I heard Michaux say this to the deacon and felt the tension in the church at Newport News that night. Still I was surprised when one daughter's marriage turned sour and members said it was the fulfillment of the Elder's prophecy.

7. *Minutes*, April 1956.

8. Ibid.

9. See *Washington Tribune*, September 7, 1933. Information on home remedies from discussion with members. One had written out a "prescription" obtained from Michaux.

10. *Minutes*, April 1955 and January 1959.

11. *Minutes*, November 1960.

12. Some members are alleged to have trumped up charges against wives and husbands so as to get a divorce and remain in the church.

13. *Minutes*, April 1953. Michaux frequently included this kind of family and social relations counsel in sermons and pulpit talks, as the author noted from her own attendance and from discussions with church members.

14. Ibid.

15. *Minutes*, November 1952.

16. Ibid., and from author's own observations and discussions with church members.

17. From *True Believer*, p. 114, and based on author's observations of members' behavior.

18. Based on ideas expressed in Hans Toch, *Social Psychology of Social Movements* (New York: Bobbs-Merrill, 1965), p. 137–38.

19. *Minutes*, November 1958.

20. *Minutes*, April 1954.

21. *Minutes*, January 1952.

22. *Minutes*, April 1954.

23. Based on author's discussions with church members and ex-members and from author's own observations.

24. *Minutes*, April 1957.

25. *Minutes*, July 1956.

26. Ibid.

27. Based on author's conversations with this couple's daughter in Hampton, Va., in 1956, and with members who had been their intimate friends and who continued in a friendly relationship with these ex-members.

28. From author's discussions with members and author's observations of such folk.

29. From author's knowledge of this church's ecclesiastical structure.

30. *Minutes*, July 1952.

31. Ibid.

32. *Minutes*, April 1954. Deacons enforced the rule by asking long-winded preachers to sit down; actually they would tug at the preacher's coattail as a signal.

33. *Minutes*, November 1953.

34. Ibid.

35. *Minutes*, July 1953.

36. *Minutes*, July 1956.

37. From interview with this former Church of God elder, in Washington, D.C., February 1979.

38. From author's taped interview with church member in Hampton, Va., in January 1972. Tape in author's possession. For earlier use of Christian, see Michaux's sermon, "Why Christians Cannot Accept the Revised Standard Version of the Bible," ca. July-November 1952; and *Minutes*, July 1952 and April 1954. For the evolving statements on why he called members saints, see *Minutes*, July 1964.

39. From author's taped interview with church member in January 1972.

40. From author's discussions with church members.

41. Based on author's discussions with church members and from author's own observations.

42. From author's discussions with church members.

43. *Happy News*, 1933; and author's own observations.

44. Based on author's discussions with church members who remembered that incident and Michaux's reaction.

45. From interview of the late editor of *Happy News*, ca. January 1972.

46. *Minutes*, January 1954.

CHAPTER 7

1. Williams, "Store-Front Church Movement," p. 83. Williams commented on having seen a copy of the telegram. For information on the contest, see "Republicans, Democrats, Thoroughbreds," in *Turf and Sport Digest*, January 1945.

2. *Washington Post*, March 2, 1940; and Green, *Secret City*, p. 239.

3. A 1946 Allen release to the press, Vertical files, Moorland-Spingarn Collection, Howard University Library; and *New York Tribune*, March 11, 1951.

4. Michaux to Mrs. Bethune, January 27, 1944, Roosevelt Papers.

5. Ibid.

6. Philip M. Klutznick, Assistant Administrator of the National Housing Administration, to Mrs. Roosevelt, February 2, 1944, Roosevelt Papers.

7. Michaux to Mrs. Bethune, January 27, 1944, Roosevelt Papers.

8. Ibid.

9. Alexander to Mrs. Roosevelt, February 4, 1944; and Klutznick to Mrs. Roosevelt, February 2, 1944, with copy to Michaux, Roosevelt Papers.

10. *New York Tribune*, March 11, 1951.

11. *Sunday Star*, November 11, 1951; and George Allen's 1946 press release, Moorland-Spingarn Collection.

12. *New York Tribune*, March 11, 1951.

13. Ibid.

14. *Washington Post*, March 12, 1951.

15. William D. Hassett, Secretary to President Truman, to James L. Dougherty, General Counsel to RFC, October 11, 1950; Dougherty to Hassett, October 13, 1950, Truman Papers. Also see *New York Tribune*, March 11, 1951, and *Washington Post*, March 12, 1951.

16. Laurence Robbins, Assistant Secretary of the Treasury, to David Kendall (an Eisenhower staff member), February 4, 1960, Eisenhower Papers; and see *Evening Star*, October 4, 1960.

17. Robbins to Kendall, February 4, 1960, Eisenhower Papers. Available information on this subject does not indicate why the Mayfair Mansions group was in arrears on loan payments and taxes.

18. *Daily News*, September 8, 1960.

19. Ibid.

20. Recorder of Deeds Files, Washington, D.C.

21. Based on discussions with church officials in Hampton and Newport News, Va., and with members of Michaux's family during the summer of 1972 in Oxonhill, Maryland, and in Newport News, Va.

22. Based on taped interview with Emmanuel C. Wright, in Philadelphia, November 1971; taped interview with Attorney Odell Walker, then Executive Director of Mayfair Mansions, in Washington, D.C., November 1971; and from interview with the former Field Representative of the church, in Newport News, Va., May 2, 1972.

23. From conversations with the former Field Representative in Newport News, Va., May 2, 1972, and in Washington, D.C., in February 1979.

24. "Elder Michaux," *Our World* 5 (January 1950), p. 44; Garnett, "Unbelievable Black Businessman," pp. 20-21; *Afro-American* (Richmond), April 3, 1970.

25. *Daily Press*, December 10, 1964, and October 2, 1968; also from discussions with the president of the board of directors in Hampton, Va., over several months in 1971 through the summer of 1972.

26. *Minutes*, November 1955.

27. *Pictorial Review*, p. 37.

28. *Evening Star*, July 12, 1938; and from author's discussions with church members.

29. *Minutes*.

30. *Minutes*, January 1955; based on author's own observations in the several churches and on author's conversations with church officers and other members.

31. *Fiftieth Anniversary Brochure, Seven Churches*, pp. 5, 25, and from author's discussions with church members.

32. In *Minutes*, November 1951, Michaux expressly stated this policy that was tradition in the Church of God.

33. I inadvertently secured this information from a secretary in the church about Michaux's manuevering to save the theater. See also the *Negro in Virginia*, Roscoe Lewis, ed., p. 346, which makes reference to Michaux's purchase of the Lincoln Theater, calling it mistakenly a "spot cash" deal.

34. From author's discussion with the secretary referred to immediately above.

35. Flickinger to Director of the National Park Service, Department of the Interior Correspondence, Colonial National Park, File No. 610, June 24, 1937. National Archives.

36. From author's taped interview with Emmanuel C. Wright, in Philadelphia, November 1971.

37. *Minutes*, January 1958.

38. *Minutes*, January 1957.

39. *Minutes*, January 1958.

40. *Minutes*, July 1958.

41. *Minutes*, November 1951.

42. *Minutes*, January 1952.

43. *Evening Star*, July 12, 1938.

44. *Journal and Guide*, September 9, 1944, p. 10.

45. *Evening Star*, July 12, 1938, and from author's discussions with church members.

46. *Minutes*, April 1956. This statement was corroborated by the former Field Representative of the church in author's taped interview, in Newport News, Va., May 2, 1972.

47. July 12, 1938.

48. From author's discussions with these former church members.

49. *Minutes*, January 1955. Frank Rasky refers to Michaux's behavior on this matter in "Harlem's Religious Zealots," *Negro Digest* (March 1950), p. 58.

50. *Happy News*, November 1933. The banker may have been referring at that time to Michaux's Pierce Arrow.

51. From author's own observations and author's discussions with church members.

52. *Washington Post*, October 13, 1956, and ibid.

53. *Minutes*, November 1955, November 1951, January 1955.

54. Robert Weaver to author, November 22, 1971, when he was Distinguished Professor of Urban Affairs at Hunter College.

55. *Minutes*, November 1955.

56. Constitution and By-Laws of the Gospel Spreading Church, Inc., November 13, 1966. Although this is the legal name of the church, it is popularly known as and referred to, even by members, as the Church of God. Note that the Elder sometimes used the name Radio Church of God for the church in Washington and in Philadelphia.

57. Garnett, " 'Most Unbelievable Black Businessman,' " *Jet*, p. 20; *Afro-American*, April 14, 1970; and based on wills of 1958, 1966, and 1968.

58. Contested will of 1968.

59. From author's discussions with church members; this matter was discussed everywhere in the church during the 1960s.

60. *Washington Afro-American*, February 17, 1973.

61. From author's discussions with church officials and with Michaux's sisters and brothers, in Newport News, Washington, D.C., and New York. York.

62. From author's discussions with church members and officials and from author's own observations.

63. Ibid.

CHAPTER 8

1. Miles Mark Fisher, "Organized Religion and the Cults," *Crisis* (January 1937), pp. 8–10, 29; and idem, "Objections to 'Cult' Classification," *Crisis* (May 1937), p. 149.

2. Donald L. Metz, "Cults: What's the Attraction?" *Your Church* (November/December 1979), p. 34.

3. *Crisis*, January 1937 and May 1937; see also Frazier, *Negro Church in America*, pp. 55–67; C. Eric Lincoln's discussion that raises questions about the Nation of Islam as a cult in *Black Muslims in America* (Boston, Mass.:

Beacon Press, 1961), pp. 212–18; newspapers and magazines from the 1930s.

4. E. David Cronon, *Black Moses* (Milwaukee, Wis.: University of Wisconsin Press, 1959); Amy Jacque Garvey, *Garvey and Garveyism* (New York: Macmillan Co., 1963); E. E. Essien-Udom, *Black Nationalism* (Chicago: University of Chicago Press, 1962); Elton C. Fax, *The Story of a Pioneer Black Nationalist* (New York: Dodd, Mead, 1972).

Louis Michaux sometimes talked about how impressed he was with Garvey and his ideas, even as a young Michaux still in Newport News. See *New York Times*, July 3, 1963; and author's conversations with Louis Michaux, in Oxonhill, Maryland, in the summer of 1972.

5. The term as applied to the black church was a creation of the 1930s. For information on Father Divine and Daddy Grace, see John W. Robinson, "A Song, a shout, and a Prayer" in *Black Experience in Religion,* C. Eric Lincoln, ed. (Garden City, N.Y.: Doubleday, Anchor Press, 1974), pp. 212–25; Arthur Fauset, *Black Gods of the Metropolis* (Philadelphia: University of Pennsylvania Press, 1944); among several books on Divine see Sarah Harris, *Father Divine: Holy Husband* (Garden City, N.Y.: Doubleday and Company, 1953); Georgia Writers' Project, *Drums and Shadows* (reprint ed., Garden City, N.Y.: Doubleday and Company, 1972).

6. Black scholars among this group are Joseph R. Washington, Jr., *Black Sects and Cults* (Garden City, N.Y.: Doubleday and Company, 1972); Frazier, *Negro Church in America*, p. 55; Raymond J. Jones, "A Comparative Study of Religious Cult Behavior Among Negroes with Special Reference to Emotional Conditioning Factors" (Master's thesis, Howard University, 1939); Fauset, *Black Gods of the Metropolis*; Robinson, "A Song, a Shout, and a Prayer," in *Black Experience in Religion.* See also J. Milton Yinger, *Religion, Society, and the Individual* (New York: Macmillan Co., 1957).

7. This quotation is taken from Franklin, *From Slavery to Freedom*, p. 276.

8. Washington, *Black Sects and Cults*, pp. 60–82.

9. Ibid., p. 17.

10. Lawrence Levine, *Black Culture and Black Consciousness* (New York: Oxford University Press, 1977), p. 43.

12. Many lay contemporaries with whom the author held discussions pointed to this as characteristic of cultists but not of leadership in organized churches, which they generally did not regard as authoritarian.

13. The Reverend D. P. Noonan, *The Passion of Fulton Sheen* (New York: Dodd, Mead, 1972), p. 67; and Metz, "Cults: What's the Attraction?" p. 43.

14. W. E. B. Du Bois, *Souls of Black Folk* (Greenwich, Conn.: Fawcett, 1961), p. 141.

15. Howard Thurman, *Footprints of a Dream* (New York: Harper and Row, 1959), p. 60–61.

16. Based on author's observations and from Fisher, "Organized Religion and the Cults," *Crisis* (January 1937), pp. 9–10.

17. Franklin, *From Slavery to Freedom*, p. 276.

18. Information from Partnership Division, Recorder of the Deeds Office, Washington, D.C.

19. Colonial File #343, National Historic Park Deed File, National Park Service.

Bibliographic Essay

I already have discussed sources of information on Elder Michaux's life in the Introduction. In addition, the following books, articles, and unpublished theses added to my understanding of the Church of God within the scope of the black church, 1919–68.

One of the earliest twentieth century studies of the "traditional" black church occurred under the auspices of W. E. B. Du Bois' Atlanta University research projects. A 1903 publication in the series, entitled *The Negro Church*, implied the irony of its approximation to mainline white Protestantism while wrestling with problems unique to recently freed black people. Carter G. Woodson's *The History of the Negro Church* (1921) and Benjamin Mays and Joseph W. Nicholson's, *The Negro's Church* (1933) are useful general studies of that institution from slavery through the early twentieth century. E. Franklin Frazier gives historical survey of the conventional church and discusses selected postmigration, black religious improvisations in his posthumously published *The Negro Church in America* (1963). In *Black Religion: The Negro and Christianity in the United States* (1964), Joseph R. Washington presents empirical and historical data on the black church. He examines it as an entity extraneous to mainstream Western Christianity. Washington reemphasized this interpretation in *Black Sects and Cults* (1972). In the latter, he classified black "traditional" religious assemblies under "sect" type.

For some of the earliest classical interpretations of church/sect typology, see Ernst Troeltsch's pioneering treatise, *Social Teaching of Christian Churches* (1921, translated by Wyon 1950) and Max Weber's *Sociology of Religion* (translated in 1961). Their works focused on religious bodies in Europe. Elmer Clark wrote a volume on *Small Sects in America* (1937, revised 1949), giving interesting, detailed descriptions of numerous such groups, both white and nonwhite. Milton Yinger, in *Religion, Society, and the Individual* (1957) and David O. Moberg, *The Church As Social Institution* (1964), following European example, apply church/sect/cult typology to interpret and classify American religious groups. These latter works most frequently are quoted, and their interpretations are adhered to too often in recent studies of "the church" in America, especially of the black component. Recent articles, such as Donald L. Metz's "Cults: What's the Attraction?" in *Your Church* (November/December 1979), raise valid questions about the relationship of the church in the United States to that in Europe and offer more reliable assessment of church/sect/cult typology in this country.

Adhering to this typology those who studied urban black religions that surfaced during the Great Depression called them cults, sects, and storefronts. One of the earliest and most perceptive studies of the religious phenomenon was printed in *Crisis* magazine (January 1937). Miles Mark Fisher wrote the article which was entitled "Organized Religion and the Cults." He discussed cults in relationship to more "conventional" churches, measuring both beside nonsexist, nonracist, and nonclassist ideals of Christianity.

Raymond A. Jones' unpublished Master's thesis, "A Comparative Study of Religious Cult Behavior Among Negroes with Special Reference to Emotional Conditioning Factors" (Howard University, 1939), employs empirical data to classify cults. In *Black Gods of the*

Metropolis (1944), Arthur Fauset identifies black religious improvisations in northern cities and classifies some as cults with variations on Jones' classification and definitions. The most recent full-length, published study on this subject is *Black Sects and Cults* (1972) by Joseph R. Washington. He refers to all black religious assemblies in the United States as either sects or cults, hybrids of American Protestantism and racism.

Father Divine has more frequently been the focus of specialized study than any other cultist. See, for example, Sarah Harris, *Father Divine: Holy Husband* (1953), Robert A. Parker, *The Incredible Messiah* (1937), Georgia Writers' Project, *Drums and Shadows* (1972 reprint) John W. Robinson's "A Song, a Shout, and a Prayer," in *Black Experience in Religion*, Lincoln, editor (1974), is the most recent presentation on Divine and Bishop (Daddy) Emmanuel C. Grace. Like previous authors, Robinson emphasizes the exotic without fresh insights although he provides important post-Grace information on program and other developments in the House of Prayer.

Since the 1960s, the Nation of Islam has been featured in several important studies. C. Eric Lincoln's *Black Muslims in America* (1961) is still the most consulted of these. In that volume, he raises important questions about the Nation of Islam as cult.

On the storefront movement of the 1920s and 1930s, refer to Ira De A. Reid, "Let Us Prey!" *Opportunity* (September 1926), and to Chancellor Williams, "The Socio-Economic Significance of the Store-Front Church Movement in the United States Since 1920" (Unpublished Ph.D. diss., American University, 1949). Williams calls Father Divine's and Bishop Grace's movements storefronts, not cults, and he supplies useful, previously unpublished information on Elder Michaux.

The preacher is a central character in black religious activity, whether he/she is lay reader, lay minister, ordained pastor. Two works that provide historical narrative on black preaching and biographical sketches of black preachers are Charles V. Hamilton's *The Black Preacher in America* (1972) and Henry Mitchell's *Black Preaching* (1970).

C. Eric Lincoln gives an update in a statement on "The Black Church Since Frazier." This is an appended section to Frazier, *The Negro Church in America* (1977). Since Michaux's death in 1968, many lively and seminal studies of black religions have been published. These deal mainly with black theology of liberation, Third World liberation, and black religious humanism. They are informative on the black church and black religious leadership more in theory and abstraction than in historical detail which I have applied to this study of Michaux.

Index

About the Author

LILLIAN ASHCRAFT WEBB has taught history at the University of Maryland and at the University of California at Santa Barbara. She is currently conducting a study of contemporary black folk prayers as a cultural form.